Dictionary of 1000
German Proverbs

With English Equivalents

HIPPOCRENE BILINGUAL PROVERBS

Dictionary of 1000 German Proverbs

With English Equivalents

Peter Mertvago

HIPPOCRENE BOOKS
New York

Copyright © 1997 by Hippocrene Books, Inc.

For information, address:
HIPPOCRENE BOOKS, INC.
171 Madison Avenue
New York, NY 10016

Cataloging-in-Publication Data
Mertvago, Peter.
    Dictionary of 1000 German proverbs : with English equi-
    valents / Peter Mertvago.
       p.   cm. — (Hippocrene bilingual proverbs)
    Includes bibliographical references and index.
    ISBN 0-7818-0471-X
    1. Proverbs. German—Dictionaries. 2. Proverbs, English-
    -Dictionaries. I. Title. II. Series
    PN6461.M46 1996   96-35554
    398.9'31—dc20   CIP

Printed in the United States of America.

To Pica
for her support

Acknowledgments

The author wishes to thank Joseph Rodgers for his invaluable assistance in preparing and proofreading the manuscript for publication, as well as his father, Constantine, for his many helpful suggestions and advice.

Introduction

Proverbs and Language—The Paremiological Minimum

Proverbs have been variously described as succinct and often didactic statements embodying the traditional wisdom of a people or as moral metaphors based on natural observation tersely summarizing experience. Cervantes characterized proverbs as short sentences based on long experience. Goethe had a strong penchant for using proverbs and by his own admission "competed with Sancho's proverbs" in his reliance on folk utterances to make his language direct and forthright.[1]

From a linguistic point of view, if languages are thought of as semiotic systems which communicate information by means of *signs* or *semeia* that stand for specific ideas, objects or situations in the real world, proverbs can be seen to function as complex units which dispense users from any need of prior formulation of concepts already current in a ready-made form in their cultural group. This is borne out by the Latin etymology of the word given by the OED: *pro* + *verbum* (word) + *ium* (collective suffix) hence meaning "a (recognized) set of words put forth."

Consequently, for a student of German or anyone else wishing to communicate effectively in the language, the most common proverbs have to be understood and learnt in the same way that idioms and individual words must be mastered. This consideration has prompted scholars in recent years to try to determine *paremiological minima* for various languages—a concept pioneered

---

1 *Goethes Werke*, Weimarer Ausgabe, Abth.IV, 292. 2f. cited in J.A. Pfeffer, *The Proverb in Goethe*, (New York: 1948), p.8.

by G.L. Permiakov in the 1970s.[2] Beginning with a vast array of Russian proverbs, proverbial and fixed expressions, Permiakov surveyed 300 Muscovites and developed a list of 1000 sayings, which he further honed down to a denominator of 300 generally-recognized Russian proverbs for Russian speakers.

In Germany, a poll of some 400 Germans of different social, professional and age groups produced 167 proverbs in answer to the question about which proverb they used most frequently, revealing that the most popular German proverb among those surveyed was *Morgenstund hat Gold im Mund* (*infra*, §553).[3] Of these 167 proverbs, 114 were recorded only once while the remaining 53 were repeated from 2 to 26 times. The questionnaire had 26 other interesting queries such as "When do you use proverbs?" "Do proverbs help to deal with certain difficult situations?" "Are more proverbs used during happy or sad situations?" The results were compiled in dozens of statistical tables and analyzed in a 198-page study that gives great insight into the use of proverbs as an integral part of cultural literacy in Germany.

In America, a comparable list of 265 English proverbs was postulated by E.D. Hirsch, though on the basis of less clear scientific criteria.[4] To determine such *minima* scientifically, extensive demographic research would be required in the form of

---

2 G.L. Permiakov, *Paremiologicheskii eksperiment*, (Moscow: 1971), and more recently in his article (1982) "On the Question of a Russian Paremiological Minimum," translated into English by J. McKenna in *Proverbium*, 6 (1989), 91-102. See also W. Mieder, "Paremiological Minimum and Cultural Literacy," in *Wise Words: Essays on the Proverb*, ed. W. Mieder, (New York: 1994), 297-316.

3 K. Hattemer and E.K. Scheuch, *Sprichwörter: Einstellung und Verwendung*, (Düsseldorf:1983). This unpublished study was commissioned by the German insurance company Aachener und Münchener Versicherung AG and was carried out by Intermarket, a marketing research firm. It is reviewed in detail by W. Mieder, "Neues zur demoskopischen Sprichwörterkunde," *Proverbium* 2:307-28. See also W.Mieder, "Moderne Sprichwörterforschung zwischen Mündlichkeit und Schriftlichkeit," in L. Röhrich & E. Lindig, eds. *Volksdichtung zwischen Mündlichkeit und Schriftlichkeit*, (Tübingen:1989), pp. 187-194.

4 E.D. Hirsch, *et al.*, *The Dictionary of Cultural Literacy: What Every American Needs to Know*, (Boston: 1988), Chapter 3, pp. 46-57.

broad-based surveys with detailed questionnaires - a painstaking labor-intensive procedure that unfortunately has not yet been systematically used in all languages, but which may now hopefully attract greater new interest with the advent of computerization and the information highway.

In the meantime, lexicological studies in Europe have shown that typically, pupils enter school with average vocabularies of the order of 2500-3000 words, by the end of 4th grade that number goes up to about 4000, and by the end of 6th grade to about 8000.[5] It is generally thought that beyond a 3000 word level a learner may become a competent reader.[6] By analogy, if one extrapolates a similar progression for those learning foreign languages, one can begin to approximate some order of magnitude of a paremiological minimum that may be required for students to communicate effectively and meaningfully with native speakers. But is any actual specific minimum figure for every language necessary or even desirable? While no one will deny that such basic minima are essential to language learning, there will never be any shortage of those who would spare no quantity of ink arguing that 300 proverbs are too few and 500 too many. So until greater documentary evidence becomes available to substantiate and fine tune the figures, the premise of the present compilation has been that the round number of 1000 should be more than enough and that a dictionary should at any rate contain more rather than less than what may actually be strictly needed.

The German Proverb

Francis Bacon said that the genius, wit and spirit of a nation can be discovered in its proverbs, and scholars through the ages have of course tried to distill a "national character" from every

5 J.P. O'Rourke, *Toward a Science of Vocabulary Development*, (Hague: 1974), p.26.

6 P. Arnaud and H. Béjoint, *Vocabulary and Applied Linguistics*, (London: Macmillan, 1992), pp.xiii and 129.

nation's proverbial wisdom. Thus German proverbs have been said to reveal a deep love for ancient beliefs coupled with the most intense rationalism and materialism,[7] while a recent provocative and excellently documented study has used oral and written folklore as well as literary sources to portray a German national character that has more than an average preoccupation with scatology.[8] But if any accurate portrait of a people is at all possible, it may be best to seek it, as Claude Roy observed, "in the juxtaposition of a nation's proverbs and *antiproverbs*, the sayings of John Doe and John Donne, the wisdom of the nation and the folly of its visionaries..."[9] Or one may conclude with Champion that "all the civilization of the ages will not eradicate the primary instincts of mankind.... proverbial wisdom is exactly the same all the world over, differing only in the rendering."[10]

This is certainly true of the proverbs of European nations which had a dual derivation: a uniform pool of human experience based on common historical and cultural antecedents and centuries of interborrowing. The German proverb therefore can be seen to be the German counterpart of similar expressions that are intrinsic to European and even universal folklore.

The main literary source for the interborrowing activity was of course Erasmus. His compilation of proverbs, entitled the *Adagiorum Collectanea*, first appeared in 1500 and was subsequently revised and expanded six times until his *Adagiorum Chiliades* was published in 1536, containing a total of 4151 *adages*, including proverbs as well as proverbial phrases or fixed expressions, a great number of which ultimately had their origin in classical antiquity and produced that rich body of medieval

7 Benas, B.L. "On the Proverbs of European Nations," *Proceedings of the Literary and Philosophical Society of Liverpool,* no.32 (1877-78), p. 316.

8 Dundes, Alan, *Life is Like a Chicken Coop Ladder. A Portrait of German Culture through Folklore,* (New York: 1984).

9 Roy, C. "La sagesse des nations" in *L'homme en question* (Paris: 1960), pp. 46-47 (translation of excerpt by the author).

10 *Racial Proverbs,* (New York: 1963), p.xxiv.

proverb lore in Latin that Friedrich Seiler, in his seminal study of German proverbs, termed *gemeinmittelalterlich*.[11] Erasmus' work quickly spawned imitations in the vernacular tongues of Europe of the time and this kind of paremiographical interborrowing has continued to this very day, to such an extent that linguists have recently coined the special term *inter-phraseologism* to refer to this internationality of proverbial language.[12] So it should come as no surprise that the German proverb *Zeit ist Geld* (*infra*, §982), which ranked 3rd in the German poll described earlier, appears to have all the earmarks of a calque of the English *time is money*.

How to Use This Book

It follows from the foregoing that this book is but a selective collection of what in the opinion of the author make up the 1000 most important and commonly used and understood proverbs of German as it spoken and written today. It is neither an exhaustive compilation nor does it include proverbs that may be current in German-speaking regions outside of Germany and Austria, as in Switzerland. This in itself would be an interesting subject for comparative study but transcends the scope of this book.

The entries have been arranged as in a dictionary, in German alphabetical order by German key word and numbered consecutively from 1 to 1000. For the purposes of this book, a *key word* is the sequentially first noun most closely associated with the meaning of the proverb and/or having a greater linguistic range or frequency. For proverbs without nouns, key words may be verbs, adjectives or adverbs used on the basis of the same considerations. Alternate variations of proverbs or alternate words

---

11 Seiler, *Deutsche Sprichwörterkunde*, (München: 1922), pp. 82-91. He catalogues 73 such proverbs with their equivalents in English and French.

12 Braun, P. and Krallmann, D., "Inter-Phraseologismen in europäischen Sprachen," *Internationale Studien zur interlingualen Lexikologie und Lexikographie*, Eds. P. Braun, Burkhard Schaeder & Johannes Volmert (Tübingen: 1990), 74-86.

or phrases used in the same proverb are placed within parentheses in the entry that represents the most common form of the proverb. An important distinction is made in providing the English equivalents of the proverbs. For many German proverbs there is an exact or nearly exact word-for-word equivalent in English where the same proverb exists in both languages in an identical or easily recognizable or closely-related alternate form. In such cases, the English proverb appears below the German entry in normal type. But where no lexically equivalent proverb exists in English, rather than provide a translation of the German, the book offers actual English proverbs[13] that would be used in similar contexts or circumstances. This is consistent with the treatment of proverbs as semiotic units that communicate entire thoughts in an encapsulated, ready-made format. Such equivalents are set in *italics* and it is assumed that the reader, once aware of the meaning or sense of a proverb and if so inclined, may proceed to identify the lexical differences by using standard monolingual or bilingual dictionaries if necessary. English proverbs that have a meaning opposite to that of the German entry are listed for comparison and marked by a dagger [†]. Cross-references are provided for similar proverbs, indicated by the symbol *cf.* An English Key Word Index is provided to facilitate the use of the book from English into German.

---

13 For the purposes of this book, English proverbs means either British or American proverbs.

Dictionary of 1000
German Proverbs

A

A	1	Wer A sagt, muß auch B sagen. Never say A without saying B. *In for a penny, in for a pound.*
Aal	2	Wer den Aal hält beim Schwanz, hat ihn weder halb noch ganz. *An eel held by the tail is not yet caught.*
Abendmahlzeit	3	Kurze Abendmahlzeit macht lange Lebenszeit. Lightest suppers make long lives.
Absicht	4	Die Absicht ist die Seele der Tat. *The intention denominates the action.*
Abt	5	Greift der Abt zum Glas, greifen die Mönche zum Krug. *As is the gander, so is the goose.* Such is the priest, such is the clerk.
Abwechslung	6	Abwechslung stärkt den Appetit. *New dishes beget new appetites.*
Abwesende	7	Der Abwesende muß Haare lassen. *The absent are always in the wrong.*
Achten	8	Wer sich nicht selber achtet, wird auch von andern nicht geachtet. *He that respects not, is not respected.*
Acker	9	Wer den Acker pflegt, den pflegt der Acker. *Keep your shop and your shop will keep you.*

Adel	10	Der Adel beweist seine Tugend im Unglück. *Adversity is the touchstone of virtue.*
Adler	11	Adler brüte keine Tauben. (Keine Elster heckt eine Taube.) Eagles don't breed doves.
	12	Ein Adler fängt keine Mücken. Eagles don't catch flies.
Advokat	13	Der beste Advokat, der schlimmste Nachbar. *A good lawyer, a bad neighbor.*
Alt	14	Die Alten zum Rat, die Jungen zur Tat. Age should think and youth should do.
	15	Keiner ist so alt, der nicht noch ein Jahr leben will; (+ keiner ist so jung, der nicht heute noch sterben kann). None so old that he hopes not for a year of life. *The old man has his death before his eyes; the young man behind his back.*
	16	Man ist so alt, wie man sich fühlt. A man is as old as he feels.
	17	Wie die Alten singen, so zwitschern auch die Jungen. *As the old cock crows, so crows the young. The young pig grunts like the old sow.*
Alter	18	Alter macht immer weiß, aber nicht immer weise. *Age makes a man white but not better.*
	19	Junges Alter ist gut, alte Jugend taugt nichts. *An old young man will be a young old man.*
Amboß	20	Ein guter Amboß fürchtet keinen Hammer. A good anvil does not fear the hammer.
Ändern	21	Ändern und bessern ist zweierlei. *Not every change is for the better.*
Anfang	22	Aller Anfang ist schwer. Every beginning is hard.

23   Guter Anfang ist halbe Arbeit.
(Frisch gewagt ist halb gewonnen.)
Well begun is half done.
Boldly ventured is half won.
A bold heart is half the battle.

24   Wie der Anfang, so das Ende.
Such beginning, such end.

Anfangen   **25**   Anfangen ist leicht, Beharren ist Kunst.
(Beharrlichkeit führt zum Ziel.)
(Wer ausharrt, hat Erfolg.)
Better never to begin than never to make an end.
Strive and succeed.
Perseverance is the keynote to success.

26   Wohl angefangen ist gut, wohl enden ist besser.
Good to begin well, better to end well.

Angriff   **27**   Angriff ist die beste Verteidigung.
A good offense is the best defense.

Anspannen   **28**   Wer sich anspannen läßt, muß ziehen.
He that has shipped the devil, must make the best of him.
If you don't like the heat, get out of the kitchen.

Antwort   **29**   Gute Antwort bricht den Zorn.
A soft answer turneth away wrath.

30   Keine Antwort (schweigen) ist auch eine Antwort.
No answer is also an answer.

Apfel   **31**   Der Apfel fällt nicht weit vom Stamm.
The apple doesn't fall far from the tree.

32   Ein fauler Apfel steckt hundert gesunde an (macht zehn).
One bad apple spoils the bunch.

33   Im schönsten Apfel steckt der Wurm.
The best cloth may have a moth in it.
There are spots even in the sun.

Appetit	34	Der Appetit kommt beim Essen.
		The appetite comes with the eating.
Arbeit	35	Erst die Arbeit, dann das Vergnügen.
		Business before pleasure.

36 Nach getaner Arbeit ist gut ruhen.
Work well done makes pleasure more fun.

37 Schmutzige Arbeit, blankes Geld.
Dirty hands make clean money.

38 Wer zuschaut, dem ist keine Arbeit zu schwer.
He that has no children, brings them up well.
Onlookers see most of the game.

39 Wie die Arbeit (der Preis), so der Lohn (die Ware).
Such work, such pay.
You get what you pay for.

40 Wo Arbeit das Haus bewacht, da kann die Armut nicht hinein.
At a workingman's house, hunger looks in but dares not enter.
Idleness is the key of beggary.

Arbeiter 41 Ein Arbeiter ist seines Lohnes wert.
The laborer is worthy of his hire.

Armer 42 Dem Armen geht viel ab, dem Geizigen alles.
Poverty wants many things, avarice all.

43 Ein Armer kennt seine Verwandten besser als ein Reicher.
The rich man knows not who is his friend.
Everyone is a kin to the rich man.

Armut 44 Armut schändet nicht—aber drückt.
Poverty is no disgrace, but it is a great inconvenience.

45 Armut tut weh.
Want of money, want of comfort.
No woe to want.

Arzt	46	Der beste Arzt ist meist der schlechteste Patient. ✓ Doctors make the worst patients.
Aufschieben	47	Aufgeschoben ist nicht aufgehoben. Delays are not denials.
Auge	48	Aus den Augen, aus dem Sinn. (Wer fortgeht, ist bald vergessen.) Out of sight, out of mind. ✓ Seldom seen (long absent), soon forgotten.
	49	Das Auge der Frau hält die Stube rein. *The eye of the master will do more work than both his hands.*
	50	Des Herrn Auge füttert das Pferd wohl (macht die Kühe fett). The master's eye makes the horse fat.
	51	Die Augen sind der Spiegel der Seele. The eyes are the mirror of the soul.
	52	Es schlafen nicht alle, die die Augen geschlossen halten. *Not all are hunters who blow the horn.*
	53	Vier Augen sehen mehr als zwei. Four eyes see more than two.
	54	Was das Auge sieht, glaubt das Herz. What the eye sees, the heart believes.
Augenblick	55	Einen versäumten Augenblick bringt kein Wunsch zurück. *A lost opportunity never returns.* Opportunities neglected are lost.
	56	Entflohener Augenblick kommt nicht zurück. *Time lost cannot be recalled.*
Ausnahme	57	Ausnahmen bestätigen die Regel. The exception confirms (proves) the rule.
Ausziehen	58	Man soll sich nicht ausziehen, ehe man schlafen geht. *Don't spread the cloth before the pot begins to boil.*

Axt 59 Mißtrauen ist eine Axt am Baum der Liebe.
Mistrust is an axe at the tree of love.

B

Bach	60	Viele Bächlein geben einen Bach.
		Little streams make big rivers.
Bart	61	Nicht der Bart macht den Mann.
		The beard does not make the philosopher.
Bauch	62	Ein voller Bauch studiert nicht gern.
		A belly full of gluttony will never study willingly.
Baum	63	Alte Bäume biegt man nicht.
		An old tree is hard to straighten.
	64	Alte Bäume soll man nicht verpflanzen.
		Old trees must not be transplanted.
	65	Der eine pflanzt den Baum, der andre ißt die Pflaum'.
		The man who plants pears is planting for his heirs. One generation plants the trees, another sits in their shade.
	66	Einem Baum soll man biegen, solange er jung ist.
		Bend the willow (twig) while it's young (green). Cf. 998
	67	Größe Bäume geben mehr Schatten als Früchte.
		Large trees give more shade than fruit.
	68	Liegt der Baum, so klaubt jedermann Holz.
		When the tree is fallen, everyone runs to it with his axe (hatchet).

Befehlen	69	Wer befehlen will, muß zuerst gehorchen gelernt haben. If you wish to command, learn to obey.
Beispiel	70	Ein gutes Beispiel ist der beste Lehrmeister. *A good example is the best sermon.*
Belohnung	71	Gute Belohnung macht willige Arbeiter. *A good paymaster never wants workmen.*
Berg	72	Je höher der Berg, desto tiefer das Tal. *The higher the mountain, the greater the descent.*
Besen	73	Neue Besen kehren gut. A new broom sweeps clean.
Bessere	74	Das Bessere ist der Feind des Guten. Best is often the enemy of the good.
Besuche	75	Kurze Besuche verlängern die Freundschaft. Short visits make long friends.
Bett	76	Früh zu Bett, früh wieder auf, macht gesund und reich in Kauf. (Arbeit, Mäßigkeit und Ruh' schließen dem Arzt die Türe zu.) *Early to bed, early to rise, makes a man healthy, wealthy and wise.*
	77	Wer sein Bett verkauft hat, muß auf Stroh schlafen. *You cannot sell the cow and have the milk.*
Betteln	78	Betteln ist besser als stehlen. Better to beg than to steal.
Betten	79	Wie man sich bettet (wie einer sein Bett macht), so schläft man (so mag er drauf liegen). As one makes his bed, so must he lie (in it).
Biegen	80	Lieber biegen als brechen. Better bend than break.
Bier	81	Bier auf Wein, das laß sein; Wein auf Bier, das rat'ich dir. *Wine on beer brings good cheer.*

Bitten	82	Bitten ist lang, Befehlen kurz.
		A long tongue has a short hand.
Blind	83	Keiner ist so blind als wer nicht sehen will.
		There are none so blind as those who will not see.
Blinde	84	Mit einem Blinden läßt sich nicht von der Farbe reden.
		A blind man is no judge of colors.
	85	Unter Blinden ist der Einäugige König.
		In the land of the blind, one-eyed are kings.
Blut	86	Blut ist dicker als Wasser (Tinte).
		Blood is thicker than water.
Borgen	87	Borgen macht Sorgen.
		Borrowing brings sorrowing.
	88	Borgen und Schmausen enden mit Grausen.
		Borrow and borrow adds up to sorrow.
Borger	89	Guter Borger (vornehme Schuldner)— schlechter Zahler.
		A good borrower makes a bad lender.
Böse	90	Bösen zu mißfallen ist so gut wie ein Lob.
		The enemies of my enemies are my friends.
	91	Böses schreibt man in Stein, Gutes in Sand.
		Good deeds are easily forgotten, bad deeds never.
Brennen	92	Was dich nicht brennt, das versuche nicht zu löschen.
		If it's not broken, don't fix it.
Brille	93	Wer nicht sehen will, dem hilft keine Brille.
		A blind man needs no looking glass.
Brot	94	Besser eigenes Brot als fremder Braten.
		Dry bread at home is better than roast meat abroad.
	95	Fremdes Brot—herbes Brot.
		Bitter is the bread of charity.

96   Trocknes Brot mit Freuden ist besser als Gebrate-
nes mit Kummer.
*Dry bread with love is better than roast meat with
fear and trembling.*

97   Wes Brot ich ess', des Lied ich sing'.
Whose bread I eat, his song I sing.

Brüderzwist   98   Brüderzwist gar heftig ist.
The wrath of brothers is the wrath of devils.

Brunnen   99   Erst wenn der Brunnen trocken ist, schätzt
man das Wasser.
We never know the worth of water till the well
runs dry.

Butter   100   Wer Butter am Kopf hat, soll nicht in die
Sonne gehen.
If your head is wax, do not walk in the sun.

D

Dieb	101	Wer einmal stiehlt, ist immer ein Dieb. *Once a thief, always a thief.*
	102	Die großen Diebe hängen die kleinen. *The big thieves hang the little ones.*
	103	Die kleinen Diebe hängt man, die großen läßt man laufen. *We hang little thieves and take off our hats to big ones.*
	104	Mit Dieben (Schalken) fängt man Diebe (Schalken). *It takes a thief (rogue) to catch a thief (rogue).*
Dienen	105	Dienen lehrt herrschen. *A good servant makes a good master.*
Ding	106	Jedes Ding hat zwei Seiten. *There are two sides to everything.*
	107	Aller gute Dinge sind drei. *All good things come in threes.*
Distel	108	Disteln sind dem Esel lieber als Rosen. *A pig used to dirt turns up its nose at rice boiled in milk.*
Doppelt	109	Doppelt gibt, wer gleich gibt. *He gives twice who gives quickly.*

Dorn   110   Wer barfuß geht, soll keine Dornen säen.
                       Barefooted men should not tread thorns.
                       He who scatters thorns, should not go barefoot.

Dreck   111   Allzu keck liegt bald im Dreck.
                       Haste trips up its own heels. Haste makes waste.

Drohen   112   Wer lange droht, macht dich nicht tot.
                       There are more men threatened than stricken.
                       Great barkers are no biters.

Dummheit   113   Dummheit und Stolz wachsen auf dem
                       gleichen Holz.
                       Ignorance and pride grow on the same wood.

                  114   Gegen Dummheit ist kein Kraut gewachsen.
                       Folly is an incurable disease.

E

Ehe	115	Die Ehe (Hierat) ist ein Hühnerhaus (Vogelhaus): der eine will hinein, der andre will hinaus.
		Marriage is like a tub of water: after a while it's not so hot.
	116	Die Ehe ist Himmel und Hölle.
		Marriage is both heaven and hell.
	117	Ehen werden im Himmel geschlossen.
		Marriages are made in Heaven.
	118	Früh Eh, früh Weh.
		Early wed, early dead.
Ehestand	119	Ehestand—Wehestand.
		(Keine Eh' ohne Weh.)
		He that has a wife, has strife.
		Cf. 198
Ehre	120	Besser arm in Ehren als reich in Schanden.
		(Arme Tugend ist besser als reiche Schande.)
		Better poor with honor than rich with shame.
	121	Lieber mit Ehren sterben, als in Schanden leben.
		Better die with honor than live with shame.
Ehrlich	122	Besser ehrlich gestorben als schändlich verdorben.
		It's better to die with honor than to live in infamy.

| Ei | 123 | Ehrlich währt am längsten. |
| | | *Honesty is the best policy.* |

| | 124 | Wer Eier haben will, muß der Henne Gackern leiden. |
| | | He that would have eggs must endure the cackling of hens. |

Eiche	125	Es fällt keine Eiche (kein Baum) vom ersten Streich.
		(Auf einen Hieb fällt kein Baum.)
		An oak (tree) is not felled at (with) one stroke.

| Eile | 126 | Eile mit Weile. |
| | | Make haste slowly. |

| Einäugig | 127 | Besser einäugig (schielen) als blind. |
| | | *Better to have one eye than be blind altogether.* |

| Einbildung | 128 | Einbildung ist auch Bildung. |
| | | *Every man has as much vanity as he is deficient in understanding.* |

| Einfall | 129 | Einfälle sind besser als Ausfälle. |
| | | *It is better to be thoughtful than thoughtless.* |

Einmal	130	Einmal ist keinmal.
		(Wer einmal trifft, der ist noch kein guter Schütze.)
		One swallow does not make a summer.

Eintracht	131	Eintracht baut das Haus (ernährt), Zwietracht reißt es nieder (verzehrt).
		A house divided against itself cannot stand.
		United we stand, divided we fall.

| | 132 | Eintracht macht stark. |
| | | In union there is strength. |

| Eisen | 133 | Schmiede das Eisen, solange es warm ist. |
| | | Strike while the iron is hot. |

| Elend | 134 | Das größte Elend ist, kein Elend tragen (zu) können. |

Elend 134 Das größte Elend ist, kein Elend tragen (zu) können.
The greatest misfortune of all is not to be able to bear misfortune.

Ende 135 Das Ende bewährt alle Dinge.
The end crowns the work.
The proof of the pudding is in the eating.

136 Ende gut, alles gut.
All's well that ends well.

Eng 137 Besser eng und wohl als weit und weh.
Better a little along than a long none.

Ente 138 Enten können nur schnattern.
What can you expect from a pig but a grunt?

Enthalt- 139 Enthaltsamkeit ist die beste Medizin.
samkeit *Abstinence is the best medicine.*

Entschluß 140 Schneller Entschluß bringt oft Verdruß.
He that soon deemeth soon repenteth.
He that passes judgment as he runs, overtakes repentance.

Erfahrenheit 142 Erfahrenheit macht Narren gescheit.
Experience is the mistress of fools.

Erfahrung 142 Erfahrung ist die beste Lehrmeisterin.
Experience is the best teacher.

Erfolg 143 Erfolg (ver)bindet, Mißerfolg trennt.
Nothing succeeds like success.

144 Der Erfolg gibt recht.
Success is never blamed.
Success makes a fool seem wise.

Ersparen 145 Ersparen ist leichter als erhalten.
There's more in saving than there is in earning.

Erst 146 Sieh erst auf Dich und die Deinen, dann schilt mich und die Meinen.
Point not at others' spots with a foul finger.

147 Wer zuerst kommt, mahlt zuerst.
First come, first served.

Ertragen 148 Ertrage und entbehre!
Bear and forbear!

Ertrinkende 149 Der Ertrinkende klammert sich (auch) an
einem Strohhalm.
A drowning man clutches at a thread (straw).

Esel 150 Der Esel hat lieber Stroh denn Gold.
An ass laden with gold still eats thistles.

151 Ein Esel nennt den andern Langohr (Sackträger).
(Es sagt ein Storch dem andern Langhals.)
One ass calls another long ears.
The snite need not the woodcock betwite.

152 Wer sich zum Esel macht, dem will jeder seine
Säcke auflegen.
Make yourself an ass and everyone will lay a
sack on you.

Essen 153 Je weniger man ißt, je länger ißt man.
He that eats least, eats most.

154 Nach dem Essen sollst du stehn oder tausend
Schritte gehn.
After dinner sit awhile, after supper walk a mile.

155 Viel Essen, viel Krankheit.
Much meat, much malady.
Many dishes make many diseases.

F

Fallen	156	Fallen ist keine Schande, aber liegen bleiben. *Our greatest glory consists not in never falling, but in rising every time we fall. Success comes in rising every time you fall.*
Faß	157	Alte Fäßer rinnen gern. *Good broth may be made in an old pot. The best wine comes out of an old vessel.*
	158	Das Faß riecht nach dem ersten Wein. *The cask savors of the first fill.*
	159	Wenn nicht viel im Faß ist, kann man auch nicht viel daraus zapfen. *You cannot take more out of a barrel than you put into it.*
Faule	160	Abends werden die Faulen fleißig. *He that rises late must trot all day.*
	161	Die Faulen und die Dreisten schrei'n am lautesten. *Idle folks have the least leisure. They complain most who suffer least.*
	162	Faule haben allzeit Feiertag. Every day is a holiday with sluggards.
Faulenzen	163	Wer nicht richtig faulenzen kann, kann auch nicht richtig arbeiten. *Work while you work, play while you play.*

| Faulpelz | 164 | Ein Faulpelz (Trägheit) (Müßigang) ist des Teufels Kopfkissen (Ruhebank). An idle person (brain) is the devil's cushion (workshop). |

Faulpelz 164 Ein Faulpelz (Trägheit) (Müßigang) ist des Teufels Kopfkissen (Ruhebank).
An idle person (brain) is the devil's cushion (workshop).

Feder 165 An den Federn erkennt man den Vogel.
Every bird is known by its feathers.

Fehler 166 Durch Fehler wird man klug.
We learn by our mistakes.

Feige 167 Der Feige droht nur, wo er sicher ist.
Any coward can fight a battle when he is sure of winning.

Feind 168 Dem fliehenden Feinde soll man goldene Brücken bauen.
For a flying enemy make a golden bridge.

169 Der ärgste Feind ist uns selber.
Every man is his own worst enemy.

Fell 170 Mann soll das Fell des Bären nicht verkaufen, ehe man ihn nicht erlegt hat.
Don't sell the skin until you have caught the bear.

Feuer 171 Feuer und Wasser sind gute Diener, aber schlechte Herren.
Fire and water are good servants but bad masters.

172 Wer ins Feuer bläst, dem fliegen die Funken in die Augen.
He who blows in the fire will get sparks in his eyes.

Fisch 173 Die große Fische fressen die kleinen.
Big fish eat little fish.

Fleiß 174 Der Jugend Fleiß, des Alters Preis.
Application in youth makes old age comfortable.

175   Ohne Fleiß kein Preis.
       (Es gibt keine Vorteil ohne Mühe.)
       Without diligence, no prize.
       (No pains, no gains.)

Fleißig   176   Für den Fleißigen hat die Woche sieben Heute,
                          für den Faulen sieben Morgen.
                          For the diligent the week has seven todays, for
                          the slothful, seven tomorrows.

Flitterwoche 177   Nach den Flitterwochen kommen die
                        Zitterwochen.
                        The honeymoon is over, now the marriage begins.

Floh   178   Je fetter der Floh, je magerer der Hund.
                          The fatter the flea, the leaner the dog.

Fluch   179   Der Fluch fällt zurück auf den Flucher.
                          Curses, like chickens, come home to roost.

                   180   Fluchen ist des Teufels Meßgeläute.
                          The man who curses prays to the devil.

Flucht   181   Besser Flucht als Leid.
                          A good run is better than a bad stand.

Fluß   182   Alle Flüsse laufen ins Meer.
                          All rivers run into the sea.

                   183   Es läuft kein Fluß den Berg hinan.
                          (Das Wasser läuft den Berg nicht hinauf.)
                          Don't try running water up a hill.
                          Water always flows down, not up.

Flüstern   184   Wo man flüstert, wird gelogen.
                          Where there is whispering, there is lying.

Flut   185   Jede Flut hat ihre Ebbe.
                          Every tide has its ebb.

Fohle   186   Die wildesten (aus klattrigen) Fohlen werden
                          die besten Pferde (schönsten Hengste).
                          The wilder the colt, the better the horse.

Fordern   **187**   Wer zu viel fordert (alles haben will), bekommt (am Ende) nichts.
Inordinate demands should meet with bold denials. All covet, all lose.

Frage   **188**   Am vielen Fragen erkennt man den Narren.
A fool can ask more questions in a minute than a wise man can answer in an hour. A fool is known by his multitude of words.

    189   Mit Fragen kommt man durch die Welt (nach Rom).
He who uses his tongue will reach his destination.

    190   Wie die Frage, so die Antwort.
Like question, like answer.

Fragen   **191**   Besser zweimal fragen (gefragt) als einmal irregehen (irregegangen).
It is better to ask twice than to go wrong once.

    192   Wer fragt, der lernt.
(Wer viel fragt, erhält viel Antwort.)
(Fragen macht klug.)
Ask questions and learn.
† *To a man full of questions, make no answer at all.*

Frau   **193**   Eine Frau kann mit der Schürze mehr aus dem Haus tragen, als der Mann mit dem Ernte-wagen einfährt.
A woman can carry out more with her apron than a man can haul in a wagon.

    194   Frauen und Geld, regieren die Welt.
Two things govern the world—women and gold.
Cf. 249

    195   Hat die Frau die Hosen an, ist der Mann ein Dummerjan.
When a man's a fool, his wife will rule.

196   Je weniger die Frau befiehlt, desto mehr ge-
       horcht ihr der Mann.
       The woman who obeys her husband rules him.
       A woman can't drive her husband, but she can lead
       him.

197   Such' dir deine Frau nicht beim Tanzen, sondern
       bei der Arbeit.
       Choose your wife on a Saturday rather than on a
       Sunday.

198   Wer Frauen hütet, wütet.
       Who has a wife, has strife.
       Cf. 119

199   Willst du eine Frau nehmen, so zieh die Ohren
       mehr als die Augen zu Rat.
       Choose a wife by your ear rather than by your
       eye.

200   Zwei Frauen in einem Haus sind ihrer drei zu-
       viel.
       Two women in the same house can never agree.

Frauenhaar   201   Ein Frauenhaar zieht mehr als ein
                     Glockenstrang.
                     One hair of a woman draws more than a team of
                     horses.

Freiheit   202   Wo viel Freiheit ist, ist viel Irrtum.
                     Too much liberty spoils all.

Freude   203   Auf Freud' folgt Leid.
                     After joy comes sorrow.
                     Sadness and gladness succeed each other.

Freund   204   Die alten Freunde die besten.
                     Old friends are best.

              205   Ein Freund in der Nähe (ein guter Nachbar) ist
                     besser als ein Bruder in der Ferne.
                     Better a neighbor near than a brother afar.
                     A friend at hand is better than a relative at a dis-
                     tance.

206   Ein Freund ist des andern Spiegel
       Our friends are our mirrors.
       One's best friend is his mirror.

207   Gute Freunde findet man nicht am Wege.
       Friendship is not to be bought at a fair.
       Real friends are few and far between.

208   Gute Freunde hab'ich viel, bis ich sie ge-
       brauchen will.
       Many friends, few helpers.
       In time of prosperity, friends will be plenty, in time
       of adversity, not one in twenty. Cf. 977

209   Jedermanns Freund ist niemands Freund.
       A friend to all is a friend to none.

210   Was der Freund bekommt ist nicht verloren.
       What a friend gets is not lost.

211   Wenn ein Freund bittet, da ist kein Morgen.
       When a friend asks, there is no tomorrow.

Freundestreue 212   Freundestreue prüft man im Sturm.
       Adversity is the touchstone (test) of friendship.

Freundlich   213   Sei freundlich gegen jedermann, dann sehen
       dich alle freundlich an.
       Be friendly and you will never want friends.
       He who would have friends must show himself
       friendly.

Freund-   214   Freundschaft ist Liebe mit Verstand.
schaft   Friendship is love with understanding.

215   Geflickte Freundschaft wird selten wieder ganz.
       A broken friendship may be soldered but will
       never be sound.

Friede   216   Ein Friede ist besser als zehn Siege.
       Better a lean peace than a fat victory.

217   Ein unbilliger Friede ist besser als ein gerechter
       Krieg.
       A bad peace is better than a good quarrel.

218   Friede düngt die Äcker.
        Peace makes plenty.

219   Friede nährt, Unfriede zehrt.
        Peace feeds, war wastes; peace breeds, war consumes.

220   Man muß Frieden schließen, solange man noch kämpfen kann.
        'Tis safest making peace with a sword in hand.

221   Wenig regieren macht guten Frieden.
        The government is best that governs least.

Fröhlichkeit   222   Fröhlichkeit und Mäßigkeit sind die besten Är-zte.
        The best physicians are Dr. Diet, Dr. Quiet and Dr. Merryman.

Frösche   223   Wo Frösche sind, da sind auch Störche.
        Where there are reeds, there is water.

Früh   224   Besser zu früh als zu spät.
        Better early than late.

Frühjahr   225   Wer im Frühjahr nicht sät, wird im Herbst nicht ernten.
        No sowing, no reaping.

Fuchs   226   Der Fuchs ändert den Pelz und behält den Schalk.
        The fox changes his skin but not his habit.

227   Der Fuchs geht nicht zum zweitenmal ins Garn.
        A fox is not caught twice in the same place.

228   Wenn der Fuchs predigt, bewahr'man die Gänse.
        When the fox preaches, beware of your geese.

229   Wer den Fuchs fangen will, muss mit den Hüh-nern aufstehen.
        He that will outwit the fox must rise early.

Funken	230	Aus einem (dem kleinsten) Funken wird leicht ein großes Feuer (wird oft der größte Brand).

Funken 230 Aus einem (dem kleinsten) Funken wird leicht
        ein großes Feuer (wird oft der größte Brand).
        A little spark kindles a great fire.

Fürst   231 Neue Fürsten (neuer König), neu(e) Gesetz(e).
        New lords, new laws.

Fuss   232 Besser mit den Füssen straucheln als mit der
        Zunge.
        Better foot slip than tongue.

Futter 233 Gutes Futter, gute Butter.
        Feed a pig and you'll have a hog.

G

Gast	234	Ein Gast ist wie ein Fisch, er bleibt nicht lange frisch.
		Fish and guests smell in three days.
	235	Ungeladener Gast ist eine Last.
		An unbidden guest is always a pest.
Gaul	236	Auch der beste Gaul stolpert einmal.
		It is a good horse that never stumbles.
	237	Einem geschenkten Gaul schaut man nicht ins Maul.
		Don't look a gift horse in the mouth.
Geben	238	Geben is seliger als nehmen.
		Better to give than to take.
Gedanke	239	Böse Gedanken zeugen böse Taten.
		Ill-doers are ill-thinkers.
	240	Der erste Gedanke ist nicht immer der beste. (Die besten Gedanken kommen hinterher.) (Erstens kommt es anders, zweitens als man denkt.)
		Second thoughts are best.
	241	Ein guter Gedanke kommt nie zu spät.
		A kind thought is never lost.
Geduld	242	Die Geduld ist aller Schmerzen Arznei.
		Patience is a plaster for all sores.

243   Geduld und Fleiß erringt den Preis.
Where force fails, skill and patience prevail.

Gefahr 244   Ist die Gefahr vorüber, lacht man den Heiligen aus.
✓ *Danger past and God is forgotten.*

Gegensatz 245   Gegensätze ziehen sich an.
✓ Opposites attract.

Geist 246   Ein gesunder Geist in einem gesunden Körper.
A sound mind in a sound body.

Geiz 247   Geiz ist die größte Armut.
A rich miser is poorer than a poor man.

Geld 248   Geld allein macht nicht glücklich.
Money can't buy happiness.

249   Geld regiert die Welt.
Money governs the world.
Money makes the world go round.
Cf. 194

250   Man muß dem Gelde gebieten, nicht gehorchen.
✓ *Money is a good servant but a bad master.*

251   Schlechtes Geld kommt immer wieder.
Bad money always comes back.

252   Wer Geld hat, hat auch Freunde.
✓ *Rich folk have many friends.*

Gelegenheit 253   Gelegenheit macht Diebe.
Opportunity makes the thief.

Gelehrte 254   Die Gelehrte, die Verkehrte.
Great scholars are not the shrewdest men.

Geleise 255   Bleib im Geleise (Gleise), so fährst du sicher.
Keep the common road and you are safe.
The beaten road is the safest.

Gemein 256   Gemein ist selten ein.
Evil seldom goes alone.

Genuß	257	Der eine hat den Genuß (die Brühe), der andre den Verdruß (die Mühe). (Der eine schlägt den Nagel ein, der andre hängt den Hut daran.) *One beats the bush and another has the bird.* *Some have the hap, others stick in the gap.*
Gerecht	258	Allzu gerecht tut unrecht. (Eng Recht ist weit Unrecht.) *Extreme justice is extreme injustice.* Much law, litle justice.
Gerechtig-keit	259	Die Gerechtigkeit bricht, wenn man sie biegt. *He that is suffered to do more than is fitting, will do more than is lawful.*
Geschenke	260	Kleine Geschenke erhalten die Freundschaft. *Friendship is a plant which must often be watered.*
Geschmack	261	Die Geschmäcker sind verschieden. Tastes differ.
	262	Jeder nach seinem Geschmack. Everyone to his taste.
	263	Über den Geschmack läßt sich nicht streiten. There is no disputing concerning tastes.
Geschrei	264	Viel Geschrei und wenig Wolle. (Große Pracht, kleine Macht.) (Große Worte, kleine Werke.) Great cry but little wool. *Great boast, small roast. Long mint, little dint.*
Gesellschaft	265	Besser allein als in schlechter Gesellschaft. Better alone than in bad company.
	266	Schlechte Gesellschaft (Beispiel) verdirbt gute Sitten. Evil communications corrupt good manners.
Gesetz	267	Neuem Gesetz folgt neuer Betrug. *Good laws spring from bad morals.*

268 Viele Gesetze—viele Übertretungen.
The more laws, the more offenders.

Gesicht 269 Ein freundlich Gesicht, das beste Gericht.
A pleasant face is the best recommendation.
Cf. 714

270 Schöne Gesichter haben viel Richter.
Beauty is in the eye of the beholder.

Gesund 271 Die Gesunden und die Kranken haben ungleiche Gedanken.
It is easy for a man in health to preach patience to the sick.

Gesundheit 272 Gesundheit ist der größte Reichtum.
Health is the best wealth.

273 Gesundheit schätzt man erst, wenn man krank wird.
Health is not valued till sickness comes.

Gewand 274 Kein Gewand kleidet schöner als Demut.
Fairest and best adorned is she whose clothing is humility.

Gewissen 275 Das Gewissen ist des Menschen Gott.
Conscience is God's presence in man.

276 Eigen Gewissen ist mehr denn tausend Zeugen.
Conscience is a thousand witnesses.

277 Ein gutes Gewissen ist ein sanftes Ruhekissen.
A clean conscience is a good pillow.

Gewohnheit 278 Gewohnheit ist die andere Natur.
Custom is a second nature.

Glashaus 279 Wer im Glashaus sitzt, soll nicht mit Steinen werfen.
People who live in glass houses shouldn't throw stones.

Glauben 280 Glauben ist leichter als Denken.
It is easier to believe than to doubt.

281   Wer leicht glaubt, wird leicht betaubt.
        He who easily believes is easily deceived.

Gleich   282   Gleich und gleich gesellt sich gern.
              (Vögel von gleichen Federn fliegen gern
              beisammen.)
              Birds of a feather flock together.

Glocke   283   Die Glocke ruft zur Kirche, kommt aber selbst
              nicht hinein.
              Bells call others, but themselves enter not into
              the church.

384   Dieselbe Glocke läutet zu Gewitter und Ho-
        chzeit.
        The same knife cuts bread and fingers.

285   Je höher die Glocke, je heller ihr Klang.
        The redder the fruit, the higher it hangs.

286   Jede Glocke hat ihren Klöppel.
        As the bell is, so is the clapper.

Glück   287   Das Glück gibt vielen zuviel, aber keinem genug.
              *Men never think their fortune too great nor their
              wit too little.*
              You can't overfill fortune's sacks.

288   Das Glück hat Flügel.
        Fortune is fickle.

289   Das Glück hilft keinem, der sich nicht selbst
        hilft.
        Fortune helps them that help themselves.

290   Glück im Spiel, Pech in der Liebe.
        Lucky at play, unlucky in love.

291   Glück und Glas, wie leicht bricht das.
        Luck and glass break easily.

292   Glück und Unglück sind zwei Nachbar.
        Fortune and misfortune are next-door neighbors.

	293	Jeder ist seines Glückes Schmied. Every man is the architect of his own fortune.
Glücklich	294	Glücklich ist, wer vergißt, was nicht mehr zu ändern ist. *Never grieve for what you cannot help.*
Gnade	295	Gnade geht vor Recht. Mercy surpasses justice.
Gold	296	Gold öffnet alle Türen, nur nicht die Himmelstür. Gold goes in at any gate except heaven's.
	297	Wenn Gold (wo Geld) redet, schweigt alle Welt (da gilt alle Rede nicht). When gold speaks, the world (everyone) is silent.
Gott	298	Dem Fleißigen (Mutigen) hilft Gott. *God reaches us good things by our own hands.* *God gives the milk, but not the pail.*
	299	Gott kommt langsam, aber wohl. *God stays long, but strikes at last.*
	300	Gott macht gesund—und der Doktor kriegt's Geld. God cures (heals) and the doctor takes the fee.
	301	Gottes mühlen mahlen langsam, aber fein. God's mills grind slowly, but exceedingly fine.
	302	Hilf dir selbst, so hilft dir Gott. God helps those who help themselves.
	303	Tu das Deine, Gott tut das Seine. *Do the likeliest, and God will do the best.*
	304	Wem Gott gibt ein Amt, dem gibt er auch Verstand. To whom God gives the task, he gives the wit.
	305	Wem Gott wohl will, dem will St. Peter nicht übel. *When it pleases not God, the saint can do little.*

306　Wo Gott eine Kirche baut, baut der Teufel eine Kapelle daneben.
Where God has a church, the devil has a chapel.

Gras　307　Indessen das Gras wächst, verhungert der Gaul.
While the grass grows, the horse starves.

Grube　308　Wer andern eine Grube gräbt, fällt selbst hinein.
He who digs a pit for others, falls into it himself.

Gut　309　Das Gute dankt sich selbst.
Virtue is its own reward.

310　Das Gute soll man nicht übergüten.
You can have too much of a good thing.

311　Großes Gut, große Sorge.
(Je mehr Geld, desto mehr Sorgen.)
(Armut macht frei.)
Much coin, much care.
Little gear (wealth), little (less) care.

312　Gut macht Mut.
Virtue is a thousand shields. Cf. 560

313　Unrecht Gut gedeiht (reichet) nicht.
(Böser Gewinn ist Schaden.)
Ill-gotten goods seldom prosper.
Ill-gotten gain is no gain at all.

314　Unrecht Gut kommt nicht auf den dritten Erben.
Ill-gotten goods thrive not to the third heir.

315　Wer nichts Gutes tut, tut schon Böses genug.
He who does no good, does evil enough.

H

Haar	316	Haar und Schaden (Unglück) wachsen alle Tage (wächst über Nacht). *Good luck disappears like our hair, bad luck lasts like our nails.*
Haben	317	Das Habich ist besser als das Hättich. ✓ *Better to have than to wish.*
	318	Hast (kannst) du was, bist (hast) du was! (Lerne was, so kannst du was.) *Who has not, is not.* *He who has an art has everywhere a part.*
Hahn	319	Ein guter Hahn wird selten fett. *Fat hens lay few eggs.*
	320	Jeder Hahn ist König auf seinem Misthaufen. ✓ *A cock is bold on his own dunghill.*
	321	Zwei Hähne auf einem Mist vertragen sich nicht. *Two sparrows on one ear of corn make an ill agreement.*
Haken	322	Was ein Haken (Häkchen) werden will, krümmt sich beizeiten. *It early pricks that will be a thorn.*
Hälfte	323	Man sollte nur die Hälfte glauben von dem, was einem erzählt wird. *You can only believe half of what you hear.*

| Hand | 324 | Kalte Hände, warme Liebe. |
| | | Cold hands, warm heart. |

| | 325 | Viele Hände machen leichte Bürde. |
| | | *Many hands make light work.* |

| Handel | 326 | Am Handel erkennt man die Ware. |
| | | *Good ware makes quick markets.* |

| | 327 | Handel ist die Mutter des Reichtums. |
| | | Trade is the mother of money. |

| Handwerk | 328 | Handwerk hat goldenen Boden. |
| | | *A useful trade is a mine of gold.* |

| Hängen | 329 | Wer hängen soll, ersäuft nicht. |
| | | Born to be hanged, never be drowned. |

| Hans | 330 | Jeder Hans findet seine Grete. |
| | | *Every Jack must have his Jill.* |

| | 331 | Was Hänschen nicht lernt, lernt Hans nimmermehr. |
| | | *What Johnny will not teach himself, Johnny will never learn.* |

| Hase | 332 | Wer zwei Hasen zugleich hetzen will, fängt gar keinen. |
| | | He who chases two hares catches neither. |

Haß	333	Wer Haß sät, kann nicht Liebe ernten.
		Seldom does the hated man end well.
		He that sows thistles shall reap prickles.

Haupt	334	Wie das Haupt, so die Glieder.
		When the head aches, all the body is the worse.
		Cf. 890

| Haus | 335 | Im Hause des Gehängten spricht man nicht vom Strick. |
| | | Name not a rope (halter) in the house of the hanged. |

| | 336 | Mein Haus ist meine Welt. |
| | | *Every home is a world in itself.* |

337   Was du hast in deinem Haus, das plaudere nicht
       vor andern aus.
       Don't wash your dirty linens in public.

Haut   338   Niemand kann aus seiner Haut heraus.
                   A man can do no more than he can.

Hehler   339   Der Hehler ist schlimmer als der Stehler.
                   The receiver is as bad as the thief.

Heilig   340   Es sind nicht alles Heilige, die in die Kirche
                   geh'n.
                   All are not saints that go to church.

Heiraten   341   Heiraten in Eile bereut man mit Weile.
                   Marry in haste, repent at leisure.

            342   Heiraten ist Lotterie.
                   Marriage is a lottery.

Henne   343   Hennen, die viel gackern, legen wenig Eier.
                   A cackling hen doesn't always lay.

            344   Kräht die Henne, piept der Hahn, steht dem
                   Haus übel an.
                   (Wo die Henne kräht und der Hahn schweigt,
                   da geht's lüderlich zu.)
                   *It's a sad house where the hen crows louder than
                   the cock.*

            345   Üble Henne, die in Nachbarshäuser legt.
                   *A good hen does not cackle in your house and lay
                   in another's.*

Herd   346   Eigener Herd ist Goldes wert.
                   A man's home is his castle.

Herr   347   Ein jeder Herr ist Kaiser (Pabst) in seinem
                   Lande.
                   (Ein jeder ist seines Gutes mächtig.)
                   Every man is a king (master) in his own house.

            348   Lieber kleiner Herr als großer Knecht.
                   Better be first in a village than second at Rome.

349 Niemand kann zwei Herren dienen.
No man can serve two masters.

350 Viele Herren, übel regiert.
Where every man is a master, the world goes to wrack.
Too many commanders cause confusion in the ranks.

351 Wie der Herr, so der Knecht.
Like master, like man.

Herz 352 Das Herz lügt nicht.
A good heart cannot lie.

Heute 353 Ein Heute ist besser denn zehn Morgen.
One today is worth two tomorrows.

354 Heute rot (König), morgen tot.
Today a man, tomorrow none.

355 Was du heute kannst besorgen, das verschiebe nicht auf morgen.
Never put off until tomorrow what you can do today.

Hilfe 356 Angebotene Hilfe (Hülfe) hat keinen Lohn.
Nothing is given as freely as advice.
Free advice is worth just what you paid for it.

Hintertür 357 Die Hintertür verdirbt das Haus.
The back door robs the house.

Hirt 358 Ein guter Hirte schiert seine Schafe, ein übler zieht ihnen das Fell ab.
A good shepherd must fleece his sheep, not flay them.

Hochmut 359 Hochmut kommt vor dem Fall(e).
Pride comes before a fall.

Hochzeit 360 Eine Hochzeit macht die andre.
One wedding makes another.

361 Man kann nicht auf zwei Hochzeiten (zugleich) tanzen.
You can't dance at two weddings with one pair of feet.

Hoffen 362 Was man hofft, glaubt man gern.
We soon believe what we desire.

Höflichkeit 363 Eine Höflichkeit ist der andern wert.
One good deed deserves another.

364 Höflichkeit kostet nichts.
Courtesy costs nothing.

Honig 365 Honig im Mund—Galle im Herzen.
A honey tongue, a heart of gall.

366 Wer Honig lecken will, muß der Bienen Stachel nicht scheuen.
If you want to gather honey, you must bear the sting of bees.

367 Wer sich zu Honig macht, den benaschen die Fliegen.
Make yourself honey and the flies will devour you.

Horcher 368 Der Horcher (Lauscher) an der Wand hört seine eig'ne Schand.
Listen at the keyhole and you'll hear bad news about yourself.

Hören 369 Wer nicht hören will, muß fühlen.
He that can't hear must feel.

Huhn 370 Geh' mit Hühnern schlafen, aber steh' mit den Hähnen auf.
Go to bed with the lamb and rise with the lark.

371 Was zum Huhn geboren ist (was von der Henne kommt), scharrt nimmer vor sicht (das gackert).
He that comes of a hen must scrape.

Hund 372 Alte Hunde ist schwer bellen lehren.
You can't teach an old dog new tricks.

373 Den letzten beißen die Hunde.
The devil takes the hindmost.
†*The foremost dog catches the hare.*

374 Der Hund ist tapfer auf seinem Mist.
Every dog is a lion at home.

375 Hunde, die (viel) bellen, beißen nicht.
A barking dog never (seldom) bites.

376 Kommt man über den Hund, so kommt man
auch über den Schwanz.
If one gets over the dog, one gets over the tail.

377 Schlafende Hunde soll man nicht wecken.
Let sleeping dogs lie.

378 Stumme Hunde unde Stille Wasser sind gefähr-
lich.
Beware of a silent dog and silent water.

379 Viele Hunde sind des Hasen Tod.
Many dogs may easily worry one hare.

380 Wenn man den Hund schlagen will, findet man
immer einen Stock.
He who has a mind to beat a dog will easily find
a stick.

381 Wer mich liebt, liebt auch meinen Hund.
Love me, love my dog.

382 Wer mit Hunden zu Bett geht, steht mit Flöhen
auf.
He who lies down with dogs will rise with fleas.

Hunger 383 Hunger ist der beste Koch (das beste Gewürz).
(Durst ist der beste Kellner.)
√ Hunger is the best cook (sauce).

384 Hunger macht Saubohnen zuckersüß.
(Durst macht aus Wasser Wein.)
Hunger makes hard beans sweet.

385   Der Hunger treibt den Wolf aus dem Busch.
Hunger fetches the wolf out of the woods.

Hüten   386   Schwer ist zu hüten, was jedermann gefällt.
Easy to keep the castle that was never besieged.

I

Irren	387	Irren ist menschlich, (+ verzeihen ist göttlich). To err is human (+ to forgive, divine).
Irrtum	388	Die Irrtümer des Arztes deckt die Erde. The doctor's errors are covered by earth.
	389	Irrtum ist kein Betrug. (Verrechnet ist nicht betrogen.) Erring is not cheating.

J

Jahr	390	Jahre lehren mehr als Bücher. Years teach more than books.

Jahr   390   Jahre lehren mehr als Bücher.
                      Years teach more than books.

Jucken   391   Wen's juckt, der kratze sich.
                      Scratch where it itches.

Jugend   392   Der Jugend Tugend gibt dem Alter Jugend.
                      (Wer sich im Alter will wärmen, muß sich in
                      der Jugend den Ofen bauen.)
                      Diligent youth makes easy age.

              393   Die Jugend soll erwerben, was das Alter verzehrt.
                      Youth must store up, age must use.

              394   Faule Jugend, lausig Alte.
                      An idle youth, a needy age.

              395   In der Jugend wild, im Alter mild.
                      Royet (wild) lads make sober men.
                      Wanton kittens make sober cats.

              396   Jugend und verlor'ne Zeit kommt nicht wieder
                      in Ewigkeit.
                      Youth comes but once in a lifetime.

              397   Wer in der Jugend nicht töricht war, wird im Alter nicht weise sein.
                      A man whose youth has no follies will in his maturity have no power.

Jugendsünde 398   Jugendsünden werden Altersschwächen.
                      Reckless youth makes rueful age.

Jung	399	Der Junge kann sterben, der Alte muß sterben. Young men may die, but old must die.
	400	Jung gelehrt, alt geehrt. *What we learn early we remember late.*
	401	Jung gewohnt, alt getan. *As the twig is bent, so the tree is inclined.*

K

Kaiser 402 Sie sind nicht alle gleich, die mit dem Kaiser reiten.
All Stuarts are not sib to the king.
All are not hunters that blow the horn.

403 Wo nichts ist, hat der Kaiser das Recht verloren.
Where nothing is, the king must lose his right.

Kalb 404 Das Kalb folgt der Kuh.
Like cow, like calf.

Kappe 405 Kappen (Kleider) (Kutten) machen keine Mönche.
The habit (cowl) does not make the monk.

Katze 406 Darf doch die Katze den Kaiser ansehen.
A cat may look at a king.

407 Gebrühte Katze scheut auch das kalte Wasser.
Scalded cats fear even cold water.

408 Hat die Katze Junge, so lernt sie mausen.
What is in the cat will come out in the kitten.

409 Hüte dich vor den Katzen, die vorn lecken und hinten kratzen.
Flatterers are cats that lick before and scratch behind.

410   Wenn die Katze nicht zu Haus ist, tanzen die
      Mäuse.
      When the cat's away, the mice will play.

Kaufen   411   Kaufe was du nicht brauchst, so wirst du bald
      verkaufen müssen, was du brauchst.
      Buy what you do not want and you will sell
      what you cannot spare.

Kaufmann   412   Jeder Kaufmann (Krämer) lobt seine Ware.
      Every peddlar praises his needles.

Kern   413   Wer den Kern essen will, muß die Nuß
      knacken.
      He that will eat the kernel must crack the nut.

Kind   414   Auch Kinder (kleine Kessel) (kleine Topfe)
      haben Ohren.
      Little children (pitchers) have (big) ears.

415   Aus Kindern werden Leute.
      Boys will be men.

4416   Ein Kind ist ein Kind.
      Boys will be boys.

417   Es ist ein kluges Kind, das seinen Vater kennt.
      It is a wise child that knows its own father.

418   Fremde Kinder werdenwohl erzogen.
      He that has no children brings them up well.

419   Gebranntes Kind scheut das Feuer.
      A burnt child dreads the fire.

420   Je mehr Kinder, desto mehr Glück.
      It takes children to make a happy home.

421   Jeder Mutter Kind ist schön.
      No mother has a homely child.

422   Kinder sind armer Leute Reichtum.
      Children are poor men's riches.

423   Kinder sind ein Geschenk Gottes.
      Children are the keys of paradise.

424 Kinder und Narren (Betrunkene) sagen die Wahrheit.
Children and fools (drunkards) speak the truth.

425 Kleine Kinder—kleine Sorgen; große Kinder—große Sorgen.
Little children, little troubles; big children, big troubles.

426 Kleine Kinder treten der Mutter auf die Kleider, große aufs Herz.
When a child is little, it pulls at your apron strings; when it gets older it pulls at your heart strings.
Little children step on your toes; big children step on your heart.

427 Man soll das Kind nicht mit dem Bade verschütten.
Don't throw out the baby with the bathwater.

428 Wenn das Kind in den Brunnen gefallen ist, deckt man ihn zu.
It's too late to cover the well when the child is drowned.

Kirche
429 Je näher der Kirche, je weiter von Gott.
The nearer the church, the farther from God.

430 Neue Kirchen und neue Wirtshäuser stehen selten leer.
New churches and new bars are well patronized.

Klagen
431 Wer am meisten klagt, fühlt sich oft am wohlsten.
They complain most who suffer least.

Kleid
432 Kleider machen Leute.
(Das Kleid macht den Mann)
Apparel makes the man.
The tailor makes the man.

	433	Kein Kleid steht einer Frau besser denn Schweigen. *Silence is the best ornament of a woman.*
Klein	434	Wer das Kleine (Geringe) nicht ehrt, ist des Großen nicht wert. *He is worth no weal that can bide no woe.*
Knabe	435	Schon im Knaben zeigt sich's an, was er einst leisten wird als Mann. *The child is the father of the man.*
Knecht	436	Wer nie Knecht war, kann kein guter Herr sein. *One must be a servant before one can be a master.*
Koch	437	Viele Köche verderben den Brei. *Too many cooks spoil the broth.*
König	438	Könige haben lange Arme. Kings have long arms.
Kopf	439	So viel Köpfe, so viel Sinne. So many heads, so many wits.
	440	Was man nicht im Kopf hat, muß man in den Beinen haben. What you haven't got in your head, you have in your feet.
Korn	441	Kein Korn ohne Spreu. *Every land has its laugh and every corn has its chaff.* *No garden without its weeds.*
	442	Wer gutes Korn sät, erhält auch gutes Brot. *He that sows good seed shall reap good corn.*
Krähe	443	Alte Krähe sind schwer zu fangen. *You cannot catch old birds with chaff.* *An old fox is not easily snared.*
	444	Eine Krähe hackt der andern die Augen nicht aus. A crow does not pick out the eye of another crow.

Krankheit	445	Die beste Krankheit taugt nichts.

Krankheit 445 Die beste Krankheit taugt nichts.
No man was ever made more healthful by a dangerous sickness (+ or came home better from a long voyage).

Kreuz 446 Hinters Kreuz versteckt sich der Teufel.
The devil lurks behind the cross.

447 Wer kein Kreuz hat, muß sich eins schnitzen.
He that has no ill fortune, is troubled with good.

Krieg 448 Besser redlicher Krieg denn elender Friede.
A just war is better than an unjust peace.

449 Im Kriege schweigt das Recht.
In wars, laws have no authority.
When the guns bark, the law is silent.

450 Krieg ist süß, den Unerfahrnen.
War is sweet to them that know it not.

451 Wer Krieg predigt, ist des Teufels Feldprediger.
Who preaches war is the devil's chaplain.

Krug 452 Der Krug geht so lange zu Wasser, bis er bricht
A pitcher that goes to the well too often is broken at last.

453 Im Krug kommen mehr um als im Krieg.
(In Wein und Bier ertrinken mehr denn im W ser.)
Bacchus has drowned more than Neptune and killed more than Mars.
Wine has drowned more men than the sea.

Küche 454 Fette Küche, magere Erbschaft.
A fat kitchen makes a lean will.

Kuh 455 Die Kühe, die am meisten brüllen, geber wenigsten Milch.
It isn't the cow that lows the most that milk the most.

456 Manch gute Kuh hat ein übel Kalb.
Many a good cow has a bad calf.

457 Schwarze Kühe geben auch weiße Milch.
A black hen always lays a white egg.

458 Wenn die Kuh den Schwanz verloren hat, merkt sie erst, wozu er gut war.
The cow knows not the value of her tail till she has lost it.

459 Wenn die Kuh gestohlen ist, sperrt man den Stall.
When the cow is stolen, they lock the barn.

Kühner 460 Dem Kühnen hilft das Glück.
Fortune favors the bold (brave).

Kummer 461 Wenn der Kummer (die Leidenschaft) tritt ins Haus (zur Tür hereintritt), die Liebe (Vernunft) fliegt zum Fenster aus (rettet sich durch das Fenster).
When want (poverty) comes in at the door, love flies out of the window. *Cf. 597*

Kunst 462 Jeder spricht am liebsten von seiner Kunst. (Jeder meint, sein Kuckuck singe besser als des andern Nachtigall.)
Every man likes his own thing best.
Every priest praises his own relics.

463 Kunst über alle Künste, seine Kunst verbergen.
The best art conceals art.

Kürze 464 In der Kürze liegt die Würze. (Kürze ist der Rede Würze.)
Brevity is the soul of wit.

L

Lachen	465	Am vielen Lachen erkennt man den Narren. *Laughter is the hiccup of a fool.*
	466	Nach Lachen kommt Weinen. *After laughter, tears.*
	467	Wer zuletzt lacht, lacht am besten. *He who laughs last, laughs best.*
Land	468	Andre Länder, andre Sitten. *Every country has its own customs.*
Lang	469	Lang ist nicht ewig. *Long is not forever.*
	470	Was lange währt, wird (endlich) gut. *Long looked for comes at last.*
Langsam	471	Langsam aber sicher. *Slow but sure.*
	472	Wer langsam geht, geht weit (kommt auch zum Ziel). *Slow and steady wins the race.*
Lassen	473	Laß nicht nach, dann kommst du hoch. *Have at it and have it. Seek till you find and you'll not lose your labor.*
Last	474	Erst die Last, dann die Rast. *From labor there shall come forth rest.* *Of sufferance comes rest.*

Laster   475   Die Laster stehlen der Tugend die Kleider.
                       Vice is often clothed in virtue's habit.

               476   Ein Laster kostet mehr denn zwei Kinder.
                       What maintains one vice will bring up two chil-
                       dren.

Laufen   477   Besser gut gelaufen als schlecht gefahren.
                       Better to ride an ass that carries me than a horse
                       that throws me.

               478   Was hilft laufen, wenn man nicht auf dem
                       richten Weg ist?
                       Speed gets you nowhere if you're headed in the
                       wrong direction.

Leben   479   Lebe als wolltest du täglich sterben, schaffe als
                       wolltest du ewig leben.
                       Plan your life as though you were going to live
                       forever, but live today as if you were going to die
                       tomorrow.

               480   Leben heißt kämpfen.
                       Life is strife.

               481   Leben ohne Ehr' ist kein Leben mehr.
                       Life ends when honor ends.

               482   Leben und leben lassen.
                       Live and let live.

               483   Leben und nichts erlangen, heißt fischen und
                       nichts fangen.
                       Life without memories is like a rare food that the
                       cook forgot to season.

               484   Man muß das Leben eben nehmen, wie das Le-
                       ben eben ist.
                       Take things as they come (as you find them).

485   Man muß leben, wie man kann, nicht wie man will.
(Wenn nicht, wie wir wollen, so doch, wie wir können.)
He that may not do as he would, must do as he can.

486   Wohl gelebt, wohl gestorben.
A good life makes a good death.

Leder   487   Aus fremdem Leder (Rohr) (Kalb) ist gut Riemen (Pfeifen) schneiden (wohlfeil pflügen).
(Aus fremden Schüsseln schmeckt's immer am besten.)
It is easy to be free at another man's cost.
He is free of horse that never had one.
The wholesomest meat is at another man's cost.

Lehrjahre   488   Lehrjahre—Schwerjahre.
There is no royal road to learning.

Leichtfer-   489   Leichtfertigkeit und Ehr' stimmen miteinander
tigkeit   schwer.
Honor and ease are seldom bedfellows.

Leiten   490   Wer sich leiten läßt, geht nicht irre.
He that will not be counseled cannot be helped.
Who will not be ruled by the rudder, must be ruled by the rock.

Lernen   491   Man lernt nie aus.
(Zum Lernen ist niemand zu alt.)
Never too late to learn.

Lesen   492   Viel lesen und nicht durchschauen ist viel essen und nicht verdauen.
To read and not to understand is to pursue and not to take.

Leute   493   Arme Leute kennt niemand.
A poor man has no friends.

494   Je mehr Leute, je mehr Glück.
The more, the merrier.

Licht   495   Man soll sein Licht nicht untern Scheffel
stellen.
Don't hide your light under a bushel.

Liebe   496   Alte Liebe rostet nicht.
Old love does not rust.

497   Der Liebe Wunden kann nur heilen, wer sie
schlug.
Love cures the very wound it makes.

498   Die Liebe geht durch den Magen.
The way to a man's heart is through his stomach.

499   Die Liebe kriecht, wo sie nicht gehen kann.
Love will creep where it may not go.

500   Eine Liebe ist der andern wert.
As good love comes as goes.

501   Letzte Liebe ist die wahre.
He who loves last, loves best.

502   Liebe bezahlt sich mit Liebe.
Love is the true reward of love.

503   Liebe erwirbt Liebe (macht Gegenliebe).
Love begets love.

504   Liebe ist (macht) blind.
Love is blind.

505   Liebe kann viel, Geld kann alles.
Love does much, money does everything.

506   Liebe überwindet alles.
Love conquers all.

507   Wer aus Liebe heiratet, hat gute Nächte und
üble Tage.
*Who marries for love without money has good
nights and sorry days.*

508   Wo Liebe fehlt, erblickt man alle Fehler.
Where there is no love, all faults are seen.

Lied	509	Ein gutes Lied darf man dreimal singen. *A good song is none the worse for being sung twice.*
	510	Neue Lieder singt man gern. *New songs are eagerly sung.*
Loch	511	Kleine Löchlein machen das Schiff voll Wasser. *A small leak will sink a great ship.*
Löffel	512	Man muß mit einem Löffel nicht zwei Suppen zugleich verkosten. *You can't dance at two weddings with one pair of feet. Cf. 361*
	513	Steck deinen Löffel nicht in andrer Leute Töpfe. *Scald not your lips in another man's pottage.*
Löwe	514	Ist der Löwe tot, so rauft ihn auch der Hase beim Bart. *Hares may pull dead lions by the beard.*
	515	Was der Löwe nicht kann, das kann der Fuchs. *If the lion's skin cannot, the fox's shall.*
Lüge	516	Eine Lüge schleppt zehn andre nach sich. *He that tells a lie must invent twenty more to maintain it.*
	517	Lügen haben kurze Beine. *A lie has no legs.*
	518	Sag' eine Lüge, so hörst du die Wahrheit. *Tell a lie and find the truth.*
Lügen	519	Wer einmal lügt, dem glaubt man nicht, und wenn er auch die Wahrheit spricht. *A liar is not believed when he speaks the truth.* *He that once deceives is ever suspected.*
	520	Wer lügen will, muß ein gut Gedächtnis haben. *A liar should have a good memory.*
Lügner	521	Zeig mir den Lügner, ich zeig dir den Dieb. *Show me a liar and I'll show you a thief.*

M

Macht   522   Macht geht vor Recht.
                     Might overcomes right.

Magen   523   Einem hungrigen Magen ist schwer zu predigen.
                     A hungry belly (stomach) has no ears.

               524   Ist der Magen satt, wird das Herze fröhlich.
                     Full stomach, contented heart.

Mann   525   Der ist ein Mann, der sich selbst regieren kann.
                     No man is free who is not master of himself.

               526   Der Mann ist das Haupt, die Frau sein Hut.
                     Man is the head, but woman turns it.

               527   Der Mann kann nicht so viel zum Tor hineinbrin-
                     gen als die Frau zum Hinterpförtchen heraustragen.
                     *A woman can throw more out the window than a
                     man can bring in at the door.*

               528   Der Mann weiß, die Frau weiß besser.
                     A man thinks he knows, but a woman knows better.

               529   Ein Mann macht keinen Tanz.
                     It takes two to tango.

               530   In jedem Mann steckt ein Kind.
                     Men are but children of a larger growth.
                     †*In the boy see the man.*

               531   Selbst ist der Mann.
                     A man makes of himself what he will.
                     A self-made man.

532 Was der Mann kann, zeigt seine Rede an.
A man is the product of his words.
A man's conversation is the mirror of his thoughts.
Your thoughts go no further than your vocabulary.

Markt 533 Auf dem Markt lernt man die Menschen (Leute) besser kennen als in der Kirche (im Tempel).
✓ *We learn not in school but in life.*

Maß 534 Wenn das Maß voll ist, so läuft's über.
When the measure is full, it runs over.

Mäßigkeit 535 Mäßigkeit ist die beste Arznei.
Temperance is the best physic.

Maul 536 Das Maul (der Mund) ist des Leibes (Bauches) Henker und Arzt.
The mouth is the executioner and the doctor of the body.

537 Mit vollem Maul (Mund) ist schlimm (bös) blasen.
A man cannot whistle and eat a meal at the same time.

Maus 538 Es ist eine schlechte Maus, die nur ein Loch weiß.
✓ *The mouse that has but one hole is soon caught.*

539 Wenn die Maus satt ist, ist das Mehl bitter.
When the cat is full, the milk tastes sour.

Medizin 540 Die bitterste Medizin ist die heilsamste.
Bitter pills may have blessed effects.

Meister 541 Es ist kein Meister geboren, er muß gemacht werden.
Masters are made, not born.

542 Jeder findet seinen Meister.
Every man has his master.

Mensch	543	Der Mensch (man) kann (alles) was er will. If you will, you can. *Nothing is impossible to a willing heart.* ✓ *Where there's a will, there's a way.*
	544	Der Mensch denkt und Gott lenkt. (Die Hoffnung ist unser, der Ausgang Gottes.) ✓ Man proposes, God disposes.
	545	Der Mensch lebt nicht vom Brot allein. ✓ Man cannot live by bread alone.
	546	Jeder Mensch hat seinen Vogel (seine Eigenheiten) (Zwickel). *Every man is mad on some point.*
	547	Man muß die Menschen nehmen, wie sie sind. Take people as you find them.
Messer	548	Ein Messer wetzt das andre. One knife sharpens another.
Mögliche	549	Wer das Mögliche erreichen will, muß das Unmögliche fordern. *A man's reach must exceed his grasp. If you want an egg, demand an ox.*
Morgen	550	Morgen ist auch (noch) ein Tag. Tomorrow is another day.
	551	Morgen, morgen, nur nicht heute, sagen alle faulen Leute. *The sluggard's convenient season never comes.*
	552	Überall geht des Morgens die Sonne auf. (In andern Landen ißt man auch Brot.) In every country the sun rises in the morning.
Morgen- stunde	553	Morgenstund' hat Gold im Mund. Morning hour has gold in its mouth.
Mücke	554	Auch die Mücke hat ihre Milz. *The fly has her spleen and the ant her gall.*
	555	Hungrige Mücken beißen schlimm. Hungry flies bite sore.

Muß	556	Muß ist (eine) harte Nuß (Buß) (ein bitter Kraut) (ein Brettnagel). Must is a hard nut to crack. *Necessity is a hard master (powerful weapon).*
Müssen	557	Was sein muß, muß sein. What will be, will be.
Müßiggang	558	Müßiggang ist aller Laster Anfang. Idleness is the root of all evil.
	559	Müßiggang ist eine schwere Arbeit. *It is more pain to do nothing than something.*
Mut	560	Guter (kecker) Mut ist die sicherste Wehr (der beste Harnisch). *Virtue is a thousand shields.* *A man of courage never wants weapons.* *Cf. 312*
Mutige	561	Dem Mutigen gehört der Welt. The world belongs to the courageous.
Mutter	562	Mit der Mutter soll beginnen, wer die Tochter will erringen. He that would the daughter win, with the mother must begin.
	563	Schau dir die Mutter an, bevor du dich mit der Tochter verlobst. *Observe the mother and take the daughter.*
Mutterliebe	564	Zuviel Mutterlieb schad't den Kindern. *A child may have too much of his mother's blessing.*

N

Nachbar   565   Auf des Nachbars Feld steht das Korn immer
                     besser.
                     Our neighbor's ground yields better corn than
                     ours.
                     *The grass is always greener on the other side of
                     the fence.*

              566   Liebe deinen Nachbarn, aber reiß den Zaun
                     nicht ein.
                     Love your neighbor, yet pull not down your
                     hedge.

              567   Mit guten Nachbarn hebt man den Zaun auf.
                     (Zwischen Nachbars Garten ist ein Zaun gut.)
                     Good fences make good neighbors.
                     A hedge between keeps friendships green.

              568   Wer gute Nachbarn hat, bekommt einen guten
                     Morgen.
                     A good neighbor, a good morrow.

Nachricht 569   Keine Nachricht, gute Nachricht.
                     No news is good news.

              570   Schlimme Nachricht (Botschaft) kommt stets
                     (immer) zu früh.
                     Bad news travels fast.

Nächste   571   Jeder ist sich selbst der Nächste.
                     Every man is nearest himself.

Nacht	572	In der (bei) Nacht sind alle Katzen (Kühe) grau (schwarz). At night all cats are gray.
	573	Je dunkler (schwärzer) die Nacht, desto (je) schöner der Tag. *A blustering night, a fair day.* *The longest night must end.*
Nagel	574	Einen Nagel schlägt man mit dem andern aus. (Ein Keil treibt den andern.) One nail (peg) drives out another.
	575	Man soll nicht alles an einem Nagel henken. Do not hang all on one nail.
Name	576	Ein guter Name (Ruf) ist besser als Reichtum (bares Geld) (ist Goldes wert) (ist ein reiches Erbteil). A good name is better than riches (is a rich heritage).
Narr	577	Ein Narr kann mehr fragen (in einer Stunde), als zehn Weise (Gescheite) beantworten können (in einem Jahr). A fool may ask more questions in an hour than a wise man can answer in seven years.
	578	Ein Narr lobt den andern. One fool praises another.
	579	Ein Narr macht zehn. One fool makes many.
	580	Eines Narren Bolzen is bald verschossen. A fool's bolt is soon shot.
	581	Man muß keinem Narren eine unfertige Arbeit zeigen. Never show a fool a half-done job.
	582	Narren sagen auch etwas wahr. A fool may sometimes speak to the purpose.

583   Narren wachsen unbegossen.
      Fools grow without watering.

584   Solange ein Narr schweigt, hält man ihn für
      klug.
      A fool who is silent is counted wise. Fools are
      wise as long as silent.

Narrenhände 585   Narrenhände beschmieren Tisch und Wände.
      White walls are fools' writing papers.

Natur   586   Natur geht über Erziehung (Gewohnheit).
      Nature is stronger than education.
      Nature passes nurture.

Neid   587   Der Neid ist des Ruhmes (Glücks) Gefährte.
      The dog of envy barks at celebrity.

588   Neid kriecht nicht in leere Scheunen.
      Envy doesn't enter an empty house.

Neiden   589   Besser beneidet als beklagt.
      Better envied than pitied.

Neu   590   Es geschieht nichts neues unter der Sonne.
      There's nothing new under the sun.

Neuerung   591   Neuerung macht Teuerung.
      Innovations are dangerous.

Nichts   592   Aus (von) nichts wird (kommt) nichts.
      Nothing comes of nothing.

593   Besser recht Nichts denn unrecht Was.
      Who does nothing can do nothing wrong.
      Better sit still than rise and fall.

594   Wer nichts hat, kann nichts verlieren (geben).
      If you have nothing, you've got nothing to lose.

Nord   595   Nord, Ost, Süd, und West, zu Haus ist's am
      best'.
      East or west, home is best.

Not   596   In der Not erkennt man die Freunde.
(Ein Freund in der Not ist ein Freund in der
Tat.)
A friend in need is a friend indeed.
A friend is never known till a man have need.

597   Klopft die Not an, macht die Liebe die Tür auf.
*When poverty comes in the door, love flies out the
window.*
*When good cheer is lacking, our friends will be
packing. Cf. 461*

598   Man muß aus der Not eine Tugend machen.
Make a virtue of necessity.

599   Not kennt (hat) kein Gebot.
Necessity knows no law.

600   Not lehrt alte Weiber springen.
Need makes the old wife trot.

601   Not macht erfinderisch.
Necessity is the mother of invention.

602   Wenn die Not am größten, ist Gottes Hilf' am
nächsten.
Man's extremity is God's opportunity.

Nüchtern   603   Was der Nüchterne denkt, redet der
Betrunkene.
What soberness conceals, drunkenness reveals.

O

Obst	604	Verbotenes Obst (verbotene Früchte) ist (sind) süß.
		Forbidden fruit is sweetest.
Ochs	605	Den Ochsen soll man bei den Hörnern nehmen, den Mann beim Worte (+ die Frau beim Rock).
		Take an ox by his horns, a man by his word.
	606	Wo keine Ochsen sind, da ist die Krippe rein.
		Where no oxen are, the crib is clean.
Ordnung	607	Ordnung hat Gott lieb.
		Cleanliness is next to godliness.
Ort	608	Nicht der Ort, das Herz macht das Gebet.
		One may change place but not change the mind.

P

Pack 609 Ein jeder hat sein Päckchen zu tragen.
Each cross has its inscription.

Papier 610 Das Papier ist geduldig.
Paper is patient.

Papst 611 Wer den Papst zum Vetter hat, kann Kardinal
wohl werden.
He whose father is judge, goes safe to his trial.

Pastor 612 Zweimal predigt der Pastor nicht.
*Don't do the same thing twice. You cannot have
two forenoons in the same day. A word to the wise
is sufficient. Cf. 929*

Pelz 613 Wasch mir den Pelz, aber mach mich nicht naß.
The cat that would eat fish must wet her feet.
You cannot have the cake and eat it.

Pfannkuchen 614 Wer Pfannkuchen essen will, muß Eier
schlagen.
*You cannot make an omelette without breaking
eggs.*

Pfarrer 615 Wie der Pfarrer, so die Gemeinde.
Like priest, like people.

Pfennig 616 Böser Pfennig kommt allzeit wieder.
A bad penny always returns (comes back).

617 Ein ersparter Pfennig ist zweimal verdient.
A penny saved is a penny earned.

618 Viele Pfennige machen einen Taler.
  Penny and penny laid up will be many.

619 Wer den Pfennig nicht ehrt, ist des Talers nicht wert.
  Who will not keep a penny shall never have many.

Pferd 620 Das ist ein dummes Pferd, das an der vollen Krippe steht und nicht frißt.
  You can lead a horse to water, but you can't make him drink.

621 Das Pferd, das am besten zieht, bekommt die meisten Schläge.
  The horse that draws best is most whipped.

622 Fremde Pferde laufen schnell.
  A hired horse tired never.
  The borrowed horse has hard feet.

623 Man muß mit den Pferden pflügen, die man hat.
  A man must plough with such oxen as he has.

624 Pferde darf man nicht verleihen.
  Lend your horse and you may have back his skin.

625 Stolpert doch ein Pferd auf vier Eisen.
  A horse may stumble that has four legs.

626 Williges Pferd soll man nicht sporen.
  (Ein gutes Pferd bedarf der Peitsche nicht.)
  Don't spur a willing horse.
  Don't whip the horse that is pulling.

Pflanze 627 Pflanze, oft versetzt, gedeiht nicht.
  A tree often transplanted, neither grows nor thrives.

Pfund 628 Ein Pfund Federn wiegt soviel wie ein Pfund Eisen.
  A pound of feathers and a pound of iron weigh the same.

Plage	629	Gemeinsame Plage (Unglück) drückt nur halb (tröstet wohl). Trouble shared is trouble halved. *Misery (trouble) loves company.*
Praxis	630	Golden die Praxis, hölzern die Theorie. *An ounce of practice is worth a pound of precept.*
Predigen	631	Andern ist gut predigen. *Nothing is given as freely as advice.* *It's easier to give advice than to take it.*
Prediger	632	Der beste Prediger ist die Zeit. *Time is the best teacher.*
	633	Viel Prediger sind, die selbst nicht hören. *Woe to the preachers who listen not to themselves.* *It is a good preacher that follows his own instructions.*
Probieren	634	Erst prob's, dann lob's. *Try before you trust.*
	635	Probieren geht über Studieren. (Lehre tut viel, das Leben mehr.) *A thimbleful of experience is worth a tubful of knowledge.* *The proof of the pudding is in the eating.*
Prophet	636	Der Prophet gilt nirgend weniger als in seinem Vaterlande. No man is a prophet in his own country.
Prozeß	637	Wer einen Prozeß führt um eine Kuh, der gibt noch eine zweite hinzu. *Go to law for a sheep and lose your cow.*

R

Rache	638	Rache macht kleines Recht zu großem Unrecht. *Two wrongs won't right a wrong.*
Rad	639	Das schlechteste Rad knarrt am lautesten. The worst wheel of the cart makes the most noise (creaks most).
Rang	640	Je höher der Rang, desto stärker der Zwang. *Higher duties mean greater responsibilities.*
Rasten	641	Wer rastet, der rostet. If you rest, you rust.
Rat	642	Ein guter Rat ist besser am Anfang als am Ende. *Advice comes too late when a thing is done.*
	643	Guter Rat kommt nie zu spät. Good advice never comes too late.
	644	Guter Rat kommt über Nacht. *Night is the mother of counsel.* *The best advice is found on the pillow.*
	645	Rat soll vor der Tat gehen. Advice should precede the act.
	646	Viele wissen guten Rat, nur der nicht, der ihn nötig hat. *Advice is something the wise don't need and the fools won't take.*

647 Was nützt der Rat, wenn er nicht befolgt wird?
He asks advice in vain who will not follow it.

Raten 648 Wem nicht zu raten ist, dem ist auch nicht zu helfen.
He who won't be advised cannot be helped.

649 Wir können andern raten, aber uns selbst nicht.
We have better counsel to give than to take.

Ratgeber 650 Ratgeber bezahlen nicht.
Advisers are not payers.

Rauch 651 Wo Rauch ist, da ist auch Feuer.
(Keine Flamme ohne Rauch.)
(Jeder Brand hat seinen Rauch.)
✓ Where there's smoke, there's fire.
Make no fire, raise no smoke.

Raupen 652 Der Raupen wegen muß man den Baum nicht umhacken.
Burn not your house to scare away the mice.

Rechnung 653 Kurze (richtige) Rechnung (macht) lange (gute) Freundschaft.
Short reckonings (accounts) make long friends.

Recht 654 Das Recht hat eine wächserne Nase.
Justice has a nose of putty—it is easily broken.

655 Wer Recht fordert, muß auch Recht pflegen.
Lawmakers should not be lawbreakers.

Rede 656 Die Rede ist des Mannes Bildnis.
Speech is the picture (index) of the mind.

Reden 657 ✓ Reden ist Silber, Schweigen ist Gold.
Speech is silver, silence is golden.

658 Wer redet was er will, muß hören was er nicht will.
He who says what he likes shall hear what he does not like.

Regen	659	Auf Regen folgt Sonnenschein. After rain comes sunshine.
	660	Kleiner Regen legt großen Wind. Small rain lays (allays) great winds.
Reich	661	Nicht wer viel hat, ist reich, sondern wer wenig bedarf. He is not rich that possesses much, but he that is content with what he has.
Reiche	662	Der Reiche hat viele Verwandte. (Dem Reichtum ist alles verwandt.) Everyone is akin to the rich man.
	663	Reiche essen, wann sie wollen, Arme, wann sie was haben. The rich man may dine when he will, the poor man when he may.
Reichtum	664	Leg deinen Reichtum nicht all auf (Lade nicht alles in) ein Schiff. Venture not all in one bottom. Don't ship all in one vessel. *Don't put all your eggs in one basket.*
	665	Reichtum allein macht nicht das Glück auf Erden. Riches alone make no man happy.
Reif	666	Was bald reif wird, wird bald faul. Early (soon) ripe, early (soon) rotten.
Reim	667	Es gibt einen Reim auf alle Dinge. *There is reason in all things.*
Reis	668	Aus einem kleinem Reis wird ein großer Baum. *Great oaks from little acorns grow.*
Reiten	669	Zum Reiten (Tanz) gehört mehr denn ein Paar Stiefel (mehr als rote Schuh). There's more to riding than a pair of boots.
Reue	670	Späte Reu ist selten treu. Late repentance is seldom worth much.

Richter	671	Ein Richter soll zwei gleiche Ohren haben. Judges should have two ears—both alike.
Riß	672	Ein kleiner Riß ist leichter zu flicken als ein großer. ✓ *A stitch in time saves nine.*
Rom	673	Alle Wege führen nach Rom. All roads lead to Rome.
	674	Rom (Köln) ist nicht an einem Tag(e) erbaut (gebaut). ✓ Rome was not built in a day.
	675	Wer nach Rom geht, lasse die Frömmigkeit zu Haus. *Don't carry coals to Newcastle.*
Rose	676	Keine Rose (ist) ohne Dornen. No rose without a thorn.
	677	Man kann nicht immer auf Rosen gehen. ✓ *Life is not a bed of roses.*
Roß	678	Das Roß wird nicht nach dem Sattel beurteilt. Don't judge a horse by its harness.
	679	Wenn man das Roß nicht schlagen darf, schlägt man auf den Sattel. He that cannot beat the horse (ass) beats the saddle.
Rühmer	680	Großer Rühmer, kleiner Tüner. ✓ Great boaster, little doer.
Rute	681	Die Rute macht aus bösen Kindern gute. ✓ *Spare the rod and spoil the child.*

S

Saat	682	Ohne Saat keine Ernte. *No sowing, no reaping.*
Sache	683	In eigner Sache kann niemand Richter sein. No one ought to be judge in his own cause.
Sack	684	Man muß den Sack verbinden, eh er voll ist. A sack is best tied before it is full.
Säen	685	Wer sät, der mäht. *What man sows, he must reap.*
Sagen	686	Sagen und tun ist zweierlei. Saying and doing are two things.
Samson	687	Samson war ein starker Mann, aber konnte nicht zahlen, eh er Geld hatte. Samson was a strong man, yet could not pay money before he had it.
Satte	688	Der Satte glaubt dem Hungrigen nicht. (Was satt ist, lobt das Fasten.) The full do not believe the hungry.
Schade	689	Des einen Schaden ist des andern Nutzen (Gewinn). One man's loss is another man's gain.
	690	Durch Schaden wird man klug. Misfortunes make us wise.

Schade	691	Wer den Schaden hat, braucht für den Spott nicht zu sorgen.

Great griefs are the medicines for our lesser sorrows.

Schaf	692	Das ist ein dummes Schaf, das dem Wolf beichtet.

It is a foolish sheep that makes the wolf his confessor.

	693	Ein räudiges Schaf steckt die ganze Herde an.

One scabbed sheep will mar a flock.

	694	Es ist ein faules Schaf, das die Wolle nicht tragen mag.

A lazy sheep thinks its wool heavy.

	695	Wenn die Schafe blöken, fällt ihnen Futter aus dem Maule.

The bleating sheep loses a mouthful.

	696	Wer sich selbst zum Schaf macht, den fressen die Wölfe (beißen die Hunde).

He that makes himself a sheep shall be eaten by the wolves.

Schale	697	In einer rauhen (harten) Schale steckt oft ein süßer (weicher) Kern.

(Je bitterer die Schale, desto süßer der Kern).
Sweetest nuts have the hardest shells.

Scham	698	Wo keine Scham ist, ist auch keine Tugend.

He who has no shame, has no honor.
Past shame, past grace.

Scheiden	699	Scheiden bringt Leiden.

Parting is such sweet sorrow.

Schein	700	Der Schein (be)trügt (lügt).

Appearances are deceiving.

Schelm	701	Ein Schelm, der Böses dabei denkt.

Evil be to him who evil thinks.

Schenken	702	Schenken tut niemand kränken.
		They are welcome that bring.
Scherz	703	Scherz will Ernst haben.
		(Aus Spaß wird Ernst).
		Half in jest, whole in earnest.
	704	Wenn der Scherz am besten ist, soll man auf-
		hören.
		When your jest is at its best, let it rest.
	705	Wer Scherz ausgibt, muß Scherz einnehmen.
		If you give a jest, you must take a jest.
Schießen	706	Nahe schießen hilft nicht, man muß treffen.
		Almost made it never made the grade.
		A miss is as good as a mile.
	707	Wer oft schießt, trifft endlich.
		He who shoots at length will hit at last.
Schiff	708	Große Schiffe können in See treiben, kleine
		müssen auf Ufer bleiben.
		Small ships may stay near the shore; large ships
		may venture more.
Schlüssel	709	Ein goldener Schlüssel öffnet alle Tore.
		A golden key opens every door.
Schmerz	710	Fremder Schmerz geht nicht ans Herz.
		It is easy to bear the misfortunes of others.
Schmieren	711	Wer gut schmiert, der gut fährt.
		(Wie man den Karren schmiert, so läuft er.)
		He who greases well, drives well.
		To make the cart go, you must grease the wheels.
Schmutz	712	Innen Schmutz, aussen Putz.
		Fair without, false within.
Schön	713	Schön währt nicht lange.
		Beauty fades like a flower.

Schönheit	714	Die Schönheit ist ein guter Empfelungsbrief. Beauty is a good letter of introduction. *A good face is a letter of recommendation.* Cf. 269
	715	Schönheit und Keuschheit sind selten beieinander. (Schön und fromm stehen selten in einem Stall.) Beauty and chastity (honesty) seldom agree.
	716	Von Schönheit kann man nicht leben. *Beauty doesn't make the pot boil.*
Schritt	717	Der erste Schritt ist der schwerste. The first step is the hardest.
	718	Der größte Schritt ist der aus der Tür. The hardest step is over the threshold.
Schuh	719	Jeder weiß selbst am besten, wo ihn der Schuh drückt. Everyone knows where his shoe pinches.
	720	Man darf alte Schuhe nicht wegwerfen ehe man neue hat. Don't throw away your old shoes before you get new ones.
Schuld	721	Alte Schuld rostet nicht. *Old sins cast long shadows.*
	722	Wer seine Schulden bezahlt, verbessert seine Güter. *He who pays his debts, enriches himself.*
Schuldige	723	Besser zehn Schuldige lossprechen als einem Unschuldigen verdammen. Better ten guilty than one innocent suffer.
Schuster	724	Der Schuster hat die schlechtesten Schuh (trägt immer die schlechtesten Stiefel). *All cobblers go barefoot.* *The shoemaker's son goes barefoot.*

725 Schuster, bleib bei deinen Leisten.
Let the cobbler stick to his last.

Schütze 726 Die besten Schützen sind, so da fehlen.
The wisest man may fall.

Schwatzen 727 Wer viel schwatzt, lügt viel.
Gossiping and lying go together.

Schwätzer 728 Unter Schwätzern ist der Schweiger der Klügste.
He who knows most, speaks least.

Schweigen 729 Schweigen ist auch eine Kunst.
He who knows how to be silent knows a great deal.

730 Schweigen ist für viel Unglück gut.
Silence in time of suffering is best.

Schwert 731 Scharfe Schwerter schneiden sehr, scharfe Zungen noch viel mehr.
Words cut more than swords.
The tongue is not steel yet it cuts.

See 732 Auf der See lernt man beten.
He that would learn to pray, let him go to the sea.

733 Lobe die See (Berge) und bleib auf dem Lande (im Tal).
Praise the sea but keep on land.

Sehen 734 Ein(mal) sehen ist besser als zehn(mal) hören. (Man glaubt einem Auge mehr als zwei Ohren.)
One eyewitness is better than ten hearsays.

735 Sehen geht über hören.
Better seen than heard.

Selbe 736 Selber tun, selber haben.
Self do, self have.

Selbst 737 Selbst getan ist bald getan.
If you want a thing well done, do it yourself.

Selbstlob 738 Selbstlob (eigenlob) stinkt!
A man's praise in his own mouth stinks.

Sitte	739	Schlechte Sitten machen gut Gesetz. Good laws proceed from bad manners.
	740	Sitte ist stärker als Recht Customs are stronger than laws.
Sommer	741	Wenn's im Sommer warm ist, so ist's im Winter kalt. Hot summer, cold winter.
Sorge	742	Kleine Sorgen machen viele Worte, große sind stumm. Small sorrows speak; great ones are silent.
Sparen	743	Spare was, dann hast du was. (Erspart ist gewonnen.) Save and have. Of saving comes having.
Spät	744	Besser spät als nie (gar nicht). Better late than never.
	745	Ein wenig zu spät ist viel zu spät. A little too late is much too late.
Spatz	746	Besser ein Spatz (Sperling) in der Hand als eine Taube auf dem Dach. Better a sparrow in the hand than a pigeon on the roof.
Spiegel	747	Schau dich zuerst selbst im Spiegel. *The best place for criticism is in front of your mirror.*
Spiel	748	Im Spiel zeigt sich der Charakter. *To find out what a man is like, find out what he does in his spare time.*
	749	Es ist ein bös Spiel, da der eine lacht und der andere weint. It is no play where one greets and another laughs.
	750	Wenn das Spiel am besten ist, soll man ablassen. It is well to leave off playing when the game is at its best.

Spielen	751	Spiel ist keine Kunst, aber aufhören. It is not clever to play (gamble), but to stop playing (gambling).
Spinnen	752	Spinnen lernt man bei (vom) Spinnen. In doing we learn.
Sprichwort	753	Sprichwort—Wahrwort. *Common proverb never (seldom) lies.* *Old saws speak truth.*
	754	Sprichwörter sind die Weisheit der Straßen. Proverbs are the wisdom of the streets.
Stall	755	Man tut den Stall zu, wenn das Pferd fortgelaufen ist. It's too late to shut the stable door after the horse has bolted.
Steigen	756	Wer hoch steigt, fällt tief. One who climbs high falls low.
Stein	757	Walzender Stein wird nicht moosig. The rolling stone gathers no moss.
Stolz	758	Stolz geht voran und Schande hintennach. Pride goes before, and shame follows after.
Strafe	759	Strafe muß sein. *Every sin brings its punishment with it.*
Streit	760	Der Liebenden Streit die Liebe erneut. (Liebeszorn ist neuer Liebeszunder.) The quarrel of lovers is the renewal of love.
Stroh	761	Wer sich zwischen Stroh und Feuer legt, verbrennt sich gern. *Who has skirts of straw, needs fear the fire.*
Strom	762	Wider den Strom ist übel schwimmen. It is ill striving against the stream.
Stuhl	763	Auf hohen Stühlen sitzt man schlecht. *He sits not sure that sits too high.*

Stunde 764 Besser eine Stunde zu früh als eine Minute zu spät.

✓ It's better to be an hour too early than a minute too late.

T

Tadeln   765   Tadeln ist leicht, aber besser machen nicht.
                    Unless you can do better, don't criticize.
                    He may find fault that cannot mend.

Tag   766   Ein guter Tag fängt morgens an.
                    You can tell the day by the morning.

              767   Ein Tag ohne Lachen ist ein verlorener Tag.
                    The most utterly lost of all days is that on which
                    you have not laughed.

              768   Ein Tag lehrt den anderen.
                    Today is the pupil of yesterday.

              769   Es ist nicht alle Tage Kirchweih.
                    Every day is not a holiday.

              770   Jeder Tag hat seinen Abend.
                    Every day has its night (+ every weal its woe).

              771   Man soll den Tag nicht vor dem Abend loben.
                    Praise a fair day at night.

              772   Womit man bei Tage umgeht, davon träumt
                    man des Nachts.
                    The net of the sleeper catches fish.
                    The pig dreams of acorns and the goose of maize.

Tasche	773	Aus leeren Taschen ist nicht zu zahlen. (Den Nackten kann man nicht ausziehen.) *If you put nothing in your purse, you can take nothing out.* *No naked man is sought after to be rifled.* *There's no use trying to strip a naked man.*
Tätigkeit	774	Tätigkeit ist das Salz des Lebens. (Arbeit ist des Lebens Würze.) *Business is the salt of life.*
Tatsachen	775	Tatsachen sind stärker als Worte. Actions speak louder than words.
Taube	776	Gebratene Tauben fliegen einem nirgends (nicht) ins Maul. *Roasted ducks don't fly into your mouth.*
Tausch	777	Tausch ist kein Raub. (Fair) exchange is no robbery.
Teil	778	Gleich Teil macht keinen Krieg. *Equality breeds no war.*
Teufel	779	Der Teufel ist nicht so schwarz, wie man ihn malt. (Die Hölle ist nicht so heiß, wie man sie macht.) The devil is not as black as he is painted. *They that be in Hell ween there is none other heaven.*
	780	Gibt (läßt) man dem Teufel (Schalk) den kleinen Finger (eine Handbreit), so nimmt er die ganze Hand (eine Elle lang). *Give the devil (a fool) (a clown) an inch and he'll take an ell (yard).*
	781	Wenn es not tut, so kann der Teufel die Schrift für sich zitieren. The devil can cite scripture for his purpose.

782   Wenn man vom Teufel (Wolfe) spricht (den Esel nennt), dann kommt er angerennt (ist er nicht weit).
Speak (talk) of the devil and he is sure to appear.
When one names the ass, he comes running.

783   Wer den Teufel im Schiff hat, der muß ihn fahren.
He that takes the devil into his boat must carry him over the sound.
He that has shipped the devil must make the best of him.

784   Wer mit dem Teufel essen will, muß einen langen Löffel haben.
He needs a long spoon that sups with the devil.

Tier   785   Jedem Tierchen sein Pläsierchen.
Every man has his hobby-horse.

Tod   786   Arm oder reich, der Tod macht alle gleich.
Death and the grave make no distinction of persons.

787   Der Tod ist das Ende aller Not (heilt alle Übel).
Death is the end of all (is a remedy for all ills).

788   Der Tod kennt keinen Kalender.
Death keeps no calendar.

789   Der Tod zahlt alle Schulden.
Death pays all debts.

790   Des einen Tod, des andern Brot.
One man's death is another man's bread.

791   Man soll keinen vor seinem Tode glücklich preisen.
Call no man happy until he is dead (before his death).

792   Wider den Tod ist kein Kraut gewachsen.
There is a remedy for all things but death.

Tonne	793	Leere Tonnen geben großen Klang. (†Volles Faß hat keinen Klang.) Empty barrels make the most noise.
Topf	794	Der Topf verweist es dem Kessel, daß er schwarz ist. The pot calls the kettle black.
	795	Jeder Topf (Flasche) findet seinen Deckel (Stöpsel). Every pot has its cover (lid).
	796	Kleine Töpfe kochen bald über. A little pot is soon hot.
Torheit	797	Alter schützt vor Torheit nicht. Old age doesn't protect from folly. *Cf.* 18
	798	Anderer Torheit bemerkt man eher als eigene. *The eye that sees all things sees not itself.*
	799	Anderer Torheit sei deine Weisheit. *Profit from the folly of others.* *One man's folly is another man's fortune.*
Tote	800	Von Toten soll man nichts Übles reden. Never speak ill of the dead.
Tränen	801	Hitzige Tränen trocknen bald. *Nothing dries sooner than tears.*
	802	Tränen bringen niemand aus dem Grabe zurück. Tears bring nobody back from the grave.
Trennung	803	Trennung frischt die Liebe auf. (Trennung einigt.) *Absence makes the heart grow fonder.*
Treppe	804	Wenn man die Treppe kehrt, fängt man oben an. *Never tear a building down from the bottom up.*
Treue	805	Die Treue ist die Schwester der Liebe. Faithfulness is the sister of love.

Trinken	806	Je mehr einer trinkt, je mehr ihn dürstet. *The more you drink, the more you want.* *Ever drunk, ever dry.*
Trockene	807	Wer im Trockenen sitzt, lacht über den Regen. *It is easy to be brave from a safe distance.*
Tropf	808	Wer einen Tropf ausschickt, dem kommt ein Narr wieder. *Send a fool to the market and a fool he will return again.*
Trübe	809	Im Trüben ist gut fischen. *It's good fishing in troubled waters.*
Trunken	810	Was einer trunken sündigt, muß er nüchtern büßen. (Trunken gestohlen, nüchtern gehängt.) *He that kills a man when he is drunk shall be hanged when he is sober.*
Tuch	811	Grobes Tuch gibt keine feinen Kleider. *You can't make a good cloak out of bad cloth.*
Tugend	812	Tugend ist der beste Adel. *Virtue is the best title of nobility.* *Virtue is the only true nobility.*
	813	Tugend und Öl schwimmen immer über Wasser. *Truth and oil are ever above.*
Tun	814	Tue recht und scheue niemand. *Do what you ought, come what may.*
	815	Was man nicht gern tut, soll man zuerst tun. *Do a thing and have done with it.*
Tür	816	Jeder fege vor seiner eigenen Tür. (Kehr erst vor deiner Tür, dann hilf dem Nachbarn.) *Sweep in front of your own door first.*

U

Übel   817   Das Übel hat auch sein Gutes.
(Jedes Böse bringt sein Gutes.)
Ill luck is good for something.
Suffer the ill and look for the good.

818   Von zweien Übeln soll man das kleinste wählen.
Of two evils, choose the lesser.

819   Wer Übel nicht straft (altes Unrecht duldet),
lädt es (neues) zu Hause.
Who rewards evil for good, evil departs not his
house. Pardon one offense and you encourage many.
He who puts up with insult invites injury.

Überfluß   820   Überfluß bringt Überdruß.
(Allzuviel ist ungesund.)
Too much of aught is good for nought.
Every extremity is a fault. Extremes are dangerous.

Übung   821   Übung macht den Meister.
Practice makes perfect.

Umgehen   822   Sage mir, mit wem du umgehst, und ich will
dir sagen, wer du bist.
Tell me with whom you travel, and I'll tell you
who you are.

Umkehren   823   Besser umkehren als irregehen.
(Wer auf halbem Wege umkehrt, irrt nur um
die Hälfte.)
It's better to turn back than to turn (go) astray.

Umstand   824   Umstände verändern die Sache.
Circumstances alter cases.

Umziehen   825   Dreimal umziehen ist so schlimm wie einmal abgebrannt.
Three removes are as bad as a fire.

Unbegonnen 826   Besser unbegonnen als unbeendigt.
Better never begin than never make an end.

Undank   827   Undank ist der Welt Lohn.
(Dankbarkeit ist dünn gesät.)
The more you do, the less thanks you get.
Of all the virtues, gratitude has the shortest memory.

Unglück   828   Alles Unglück ist gut, wenn man Brot dabei hat.
All griefs with bread are less.

829   Das Unglück (Krankheit) kommt zu Pferd und geht zu Fuß(e weg).
Misfortune (sickness) arrives on horseback but departs on foot.

830   Es kommt kein Unglück allein.
Misfortunes (misery) (troubles) never come(s) singly (alone).

831   Gegen (wider) Unglück gibt's (hilft) keine Medizin (Kunst).
No fence against ill fortune (a flail).

832   Kein Unglück (ist) so groß (es ist selten ein Schaden), es hat (s)ein Glück im Schoß (dabei) (es ist ein Nutzen dabei).
There is nothing so bad in which there is not something good.
Every cloud has a silver lining.

833   Unglück kommt ungerufen
Sorrow comes unsent for.

834   Wenn ein Unglück sein soll, so kannst du auf
        den Rücken fallen und die Nas abbrechen.
        *The man born to misfortune will fall on his back
        and fracture his nose.*

Unkraut   835   Unkraut vergeht nicht.
                    Ill weeds grow apace.

836   Unkraut wächst ungesät.
        Weeds want no sowing.

837   Wer Unkraut sät, kann keinen Weizen ernten.
        You can't get grain by sowing grass.

Unnützes   838   Unnützes, noch so billig gekauft, ist immer zu
                    teuer gekauft.
                    A thing you don't want is dear at any price.

Unrecht   839   Besser Unrecht leiden, als Unrecht tun.
                    It is better to suffer wrong (an injury) than to
                    do (inflict) wrong (one).

Untreue   840   Untreue wird mit Untreue bezahlt.
                    *Those who betray their friends must not expect
                    others to keep faith with them.*

Unverhofft 841   Unverhofft kommt oft.
                    (Es kommt oft anders, als man denkt.)
                    The unexpected often (always) happens.

Ursache   842   Kleine Ursache, grosse Wirkungen.
                    Little subjects decide big ones.

V

Vater	843	Ein Vater ernährt eher zehn Kinder als zehn Kinder einen Vater.

One father is enough to govern a hundred sons, but not a hundred sons one father.

844 Mit Vater und Mutter soll man nicht streiten.
Honor your father and mother.

845 Was der Vater erspart, vertut der Sohn.
A miserly father makes a prodigal son.

Vaterland 846 Wo es mir wohlgeht, da ist mein Vaterland.
Where it is well with me, there is my country.

Verdacht 847 Verdacht ist der Freundschaft Gift.
Love cannot dwell with suspicion.

Verduß 848 Ohne Verdruß ist kein Genuß.
No joy without annoy.

Vergeben 849 Vergeben ist nicht vergessen.
It is easier to forgive than to forget.

850 Vergib (verzeih) dir nichts, den andern viel.
Forgive yourself nothing and others much.

Vergleich 851 Ein magerer Vergleich ist besser als ein fetter Prozeß.
A lean (ill) agreement is better than a fat (good) judgment.

852 Vergleiche hinken.
Comparisons are odious.

Verheißen	853	Verheißen (versprechen) macht Schuld(en). A promise is a debt.
	854	Verheißen bindet Narren. *Fools rejoice at promises.*
Verlassen	855	Wer sich auf andere verläßt, ist verlassen. *He who depends on another dines ill and sups worse.*
Verletzen	856	Verletzen ist leicht, heilen schwer. *One is not so soon healed than hurt.*
Verlierer	857	Der Verlierer hat immer Unrecht. Losers are always in the wrong.
Verlobt	858	Verlobt ist noch nicht verheiratet. There's many a slip 'twixt the cup and the lip. *Between promising and performing, a man may marry his daughter. Cf. 1000*
Verschieben	859	Verschiebe nicht auf morgen, was du heute kannst besorgen. Don't put off for tomorrow what you can do today.
Versehen	860	Versehen ist kein Vergehen. *Every slip is not a fall.*
Ver-sprechen (n)	861	Versprechen füllt den Magen nicht. Promises don't fill the belly.
Ver-sprechen (v)	862	Leicht versprochen, leicht gebrochen. *A promise is made to be broken.*
	863	Versprechen und halten sind zweierlei. It is one thing to promise, another to perform.
	864	Wer nichts verspricht, braucht nichts zu halten. Who makes no promises has none to perform.
	865	Wer schnell verspricht, der bald vergißt. (Schnell versprochen, bald vergessen.) Men apt to promise are apt to forget.

	866	Wer viel verspricht, hält wenig.
		Expect nothing from him who promises a great deal.
Verstand	867	Verstand und Schönheit sind selten beisammen.
		Beauty has no brains.
Verteidigen	868	Wer sich verteidigt, klagt sich an.
		Who excuses himself, accuses himself.
Vertrauen	869	Vertrauen erweckt Vertrauen.
		Confidence begets confidence.
	870	Wo kein Vertrauen, da ist auch keine Treue.
		Trust is dead, ill payment killed it.
		He who trusts not, is not deceived.
Vertraulich-keit	871	Allzu große Vertraulichkeit erzeugt Verachtung.
		Familiarity breeds contempt.
Verzeihung	872	Verzeihung (Verzeihen) ist die beste Rache.
		The noblest revenge is to forgive.
Viel	873	Viele können mehr denn einer.
		Many hands make light work.
Vogel	874	Alte Vögel lassen sich schwer rupfen.
		The older the bird the more unwillingly it parts with its feathers.
	875	Besser ein Vogel in der Hand (Schüssel) (im Netz) als zehn am Strand (in der Luft) (in der Weite).
		A bird in the hand (platter) (sack) is worth two (ten) in the bush. *Cf.* 746
	876	Böser Vogel (Wurzel), böses Ei (üble Frucht).
		Bad bird, bad eggs.
		Of evil grain, no good seed can come.
	877	Das ist ein schlechter Vogel, der das eigne Nest beschmutzt.
		It's an ill bird that fouls its own nest.

878 Jeder (jedem) Vogel hat sein Nest lieb (gefällt sein Nest).
Each bird likes its own nest best.

879 Kein Vogel fliegt so hoch, er kommt wieder auf die Erde.
A bird never flies so high that it doesn't touch the ground.
Every high-flying bird must at some time alight.

880 Kleine Vöglein, kleine Nestlein.
Little bird, little nest.

881 Man kennt den Vogel an den Federn.
Every bird is known by its feathers.

882 Nach und nach macht der Vogel sein Nest.
Little by little the bird builds its nest.

Volk 883 Volkes Stimme, Gottes Stimme.
The voice of the people, the voice of God.

Voll 884 Voll macht faul.
When the belly is full, the bones are at rest.
A full belly neither flies nor fights well.

Vorbeugen 885 Vorbeugen ist besser als Heilen.
(Einen Schaden verhüten ist besser als ihn heilen.)
Prevention is better than cure.

Vorsicht 886 Vorsicht ist die Mutter der Weisheit.
Caution is the parent of safety.
Caution is the eldest child of wisdom.

Vorsorge 887 Vorsorge verhütet Nachsorge.
(Vorsicht ist besser als Nachsicht.)
He that looks not before, finds himself behind.
A stitch in time saves nine.

Vorteil 888 Kein Vorteil ohne (seinen) Nachteil.
Every commodity has its discommodity.

Vorurteile 889 Vorurteile sind immer Zeichen von Schwäche. *When the judgment is weak, the prejudice is strong.*

W

Wagen (n)	890	Der Wagen muß gehen, wie ihn die Pferde führen. *When the crow flies, her tail follows.* *Cf. 334*
Wagen (v)	891	Wer (nicht) wagt, (der nicht) gewinnt. *No risk, no gain.* *Nothing ventured, nothing gained.*
Wägen	892	Erst wägen (besinn's), dann wagen (beginn's). *Think—then act. Think (look) before you leap.* *Think on the end before you begin.*
Wahl	893	Wer die Wahl hat, hat die Qual. *He that has a choice has trouble.*
Wahrheit	894	Die Wahrheit liegt in der Mitte. *Virtue is found in the middle.*
	895	Die Wahrheit will an den Tag. *The truth will out (come to light).*
	896	Die Wahrheit wird alt, aber sie stirbt nicht. *Truth never perishes.*
	897	Man kann die Wahrheit drücken, aber nicht erdrücken. *The truth, crushed to earth, will rise again.*
	898	Wahrheit ist der Zeit Tochter. Truth is the daughter of time.

899   Wahrheit sagt den Text ohne Glossen.
The language of truth is simple.

900   Wer die Wahrheit redet, findet keine Herberge.
He who speaks the truth must have one foot in the stirrup.

901   Wer will die Wahrheit sagen, muß schnell von dannen jagen.
Speak the truth and run.

Wand   902   Wände haben Ohren (+ Fenster Augen).
Walls have ears (+ *and the plain has eyes*).

Ware   903   Gute Ware (Werk) lobt sich selbst.
Pleasing ware is half sold.
Good wine needs no bush.

Warten   904   Lang warten ist nicht geschenkt.
A gift much expected is paid, not given.
To refuse and give tardily is all the same.

Warum   905   Jedes Warum hat sein Darum.
Every why has wherefore.

Wasser   906   Bei (mit) Wasser und Brot, wird man nicht tot (kommt man durch alle Not).
Eat bread and drink water, and you will live a long life.

907   Das Wasser ist am besten an der Quelle.
The fountain is clearest at its source.

908   In großen Wassern fängt man grosse Fische.
Great fishes are caught in great waters.

909   Man muß unreines Wasser nicht eher weggießen, bis man reines hat.
Don't throw away (cast not out) dirty (the foul) water until you get clean.

910   Stille Wasser sind (gründen) tief.
Still waters run deep.

Wasserkrug	911	Wasserkrug macht alt und klug.

Water is the only drink for a wise man.

Weg	912	Auf der Weg, den viele gehn, wächst kein Gras.

A trodden path bears no grass.
Grass doesn't grow on a busy street.

913 Der gerade Weg ist der beste.
Follow the straight road. Stay on the straight and narrow path.

914 Kein Weg ist lang mit einem guten Freund als Begleiter.
(Freunde sind gut am Wege.)
(Gut' Gespräch kürzt den Weg.)
No road is long with good company.
Cheerful (pleasant) company shortens the miles.
A good companion is a wagon in the way.

915 Kein Weg ist zu weit, wenn die Liebe treibt.
For a good friend (to a friend's house), the journey (trail) is never too long.

Weib 916 Dein Weib, dein Schwert, und dein Pferd magst du wohl zeigen aber nichts ausleihen.
A horse, a wife, and a sword may be shewed, but not lent.

917 Drei Weiber (Frauen), drei Gänse und drei Frösche machen (dreier Weiber Gezänk macht) einen Jahrmarkt.
Three women and a goose make a market.

918 Ein Weib verschweigt was sie nicht weiß.
A woman conceals what she knows not.

919 Weib und Leinwand kauft man nicht bei Lichte.
Choose neither a woman nor linen by candle-light.

920 Weiber sind veränderlich wie Aprilwetter.
Women are as fickle as April weather.

Weichen 921 Es ist besser weichen als zanken.
Yielding stills all war. It is better to yield than to come to misfortune through stubborness.

922 Wer weicht, kann ein andermal schlagen.
He that fights and runs away may live to fight another day.

Wein 923 Der Wein ist die Milch der Alten.
Wine is old man's milk.

924 Wein trinken, Wein bezahlen.
Sweet is the wine, but sour's the payment.

925 Wein sagt die Wahrheit (ist ein Wahrsager).
In wine there is truth.

926 Wenn der Wein eingeht, geht der Mund auf.
When wine sinks, words swim.

927 Wer trunken wird, ist schuldig, nicht der Wein.
Intoxication is not the wine's fault, but the man's.

928 Wo Wein eingeht, da geht der Witz (Scham) aus.
(Ist das Bier/der Wein im Manne, ist der Verstand in der Kanne.)
When wine is in, wit is out.

Weise 929 Dem Weisen genügt ein Word.
A word to the wise is sufficient. *Cf. 612*

930 Der Weise hat Vorteil in allen Landen.
A wise man esteems every place to be his country.

931 Der Weise tut das am Anfang, was der Narr am Ende tut.
What the fool does in the end, the wise man does in the beginning.

932 Zu Weise ist Narrei (Torheit).
No man is always wise.
It takes a wise man to be a fool.

Welt	933	Also geht es in der Welt; der eine steigt, der andre fällt. *The world is a ladder for some to go up and some down.*
	934	Nichts ist vollkommen auf der Welt. *Nothing is perfect.*
	935	Nimm die Welt, wie sie ist, nicht wie sie sein sollte. *Take things as they are, not as you'd have them be.*
Wenig	936	Viele Wenig (Federn) machen ein Viel (Bett). Many smalls (littles) make a great (lot). *Many drops make a shower.*
	937	Wenig zu wenig (wenig und oft) macht zuletzt viel. *Little and often fills the purse.*
Wenn	938	Wenn das Wörtchen wenn nicht wär', wär' mein Vater Millionär (Ratsherr) (wäre mancher Bauer ein Edelmann). ✓*If it wasn't for the "ifs," you'd be rich.* *If "ifs" and "ands" were pots and pans, there'd be no trade for tinkers.* ✓*If my aunt had been a man, she'd have been my uncle.*
Werk	939	Das Werk lobt den Meister. Work commends the master.
Werkleute	940	Werkleute findet man leichter als Meister. Workmen are easier found than masters.
Wetter	941	Bei gutem Wetter kann jeder Steuermann sein. (Wenn's Schiff gut geht, will jeder Schiffsherr sein.) In a calm sea every man is a pilot. In calm waters, every ship has a good captain.
Wie	942	Wie (weichst) du mir, so (weich) ich dir. ✓*Scratch my back and I'll scratch yours.* Tit for tat.

Wiege   943   Mancher sorgt für die Wiege, ehe das Kind geboren ist.
Boil not the pap before the child is born.

Wille   944   Des Menschen Wille ist sein Himmelreich.
A man's will is his heaven.

   945   Wo ein Wille ist, da ist auch ein Weg.
(Willenskraft Wege schafft.)
Where there's a will there's a way.

Wind   946   Großer Wind bringt oft nur kleinen (ist selten ohne) Regen.
When the thunder is very loud, there's very little rain.

   947   Wer wind sät, wird Sturm ernten.
Sow the wind and reap the whirlwind.

Winnen   948   Wie gewonnen, so zerronnen.
Easy come, easy go.
You win a few and you lose a few.

Wirt   949   Er fragt den Wirt, ob er guten Wein hat.
Ask mine host whether he has good wine.

Wissen   950   Was drei wissen, wissen hundert.
It is no secret that is known to three.

   951   Was ich nicht weiß, macht mich nicht heiß.
What I don't know, won't hurt me.

   952   Wer nichts weiß, dem entfällt auch nichts.
What one doesn't know won't hurt him.

Wohltat   953   Wohltat annehmen ist Freiheit verkaufen.
When you accept a benefit, you sell your freedom.

Wolf   954   Dem schlafenden Wolf läuft kein Schaf ins Maul.
The sleeping fox catches no poultry.

955   Der Wolf frißt auch die gezählten (gezeichneten) Schafe.
The wolf eats often of the sheep that have been told (counted).

956   Der Wölfe Tod ist der Schafe Heil.
The death of the wolves is the safety of the sheep. *Cf.* 959

957   Der Wolf wird älter, aber nicht besser.
The fox may grow grey, but never good.

958   Wenn man unter den Wölfen ist, muß man mit ihnen heulen.
(Mit den Wölfen muß man heulen.)
Who keeps company with wolves learns to howl.

959   Wer des Wolfes schont, der gefährdet die Schafe.
The life of the wolf is the death of the lamb.
Cf. 956

Wort   960   Gute Worte und harte Strafen sind die beste Zucht.
Reward and punishment are the walls of a city.

961   Schöne (höfliche) Worte helfen (vermögen) viel und kosten wenig.
(Dankberkeit kostet nichts und tut Gott und Menschen wohl.)
Pleasant words are valued and do not cost much.
Politeness costs nothing and gains everything.

962   Von Worten zu Taten (Werken) ist ein weiter Weg.
From word to deed is a great space.

963   Worte zahlen keinen Zoll.
Talking pays no toll.

Wunde   964   Alte Wunden bluten leicht.
Old wounds soon bleed.

965   Auch geheilte Wunden lassen Narben zurück.
(Narben bleiben, auch wenn die Wunden ver-
heilen.)
Though the wound be healed, the scar remains.

Wunsch   966   Der Wunsch is oft Vater des Gedenkens.
The wish is father to the thought.

967   Es gehen viele Wünsche in einem Sack.
Wishes never fill the bag.

Wünschen   968   Wenn Wünschen hülfe, wären alle reich.
If wishes were horses, beggars might ride.

969   Wer viel wünscht, dem fehlt viel.
Much would have more.
He is not poor that has little, but he that desires much.

Wurm   970   Wenn man den Wurm tritt, so krümmt er sich.
Tread on a worm and it will turn.

Wurst   971   Wurst wider Wurst.
Tit for tat.
What's sauce for the goose is sauce for the gander.

Z

Zank	972	Zum Zanken gehören immer zwei. It takes two to quarrel.
Zeit	973	Alles zu seiner Zeit. Everything has its time.
	974	Andere Zeiten, andere Sitten. Other times, other customs.
	975	Die Zeit heilt alle Wunden. Time heals all wounds.
	976	Die Zeit frißt alles. Time devours all things. *Cf.* 208
	977	In böser Zeit sind Freunde weit. *When good cheer is lacking, our friends will be packing.*
	978	Kommt Zeit, kommt Rat. (Zeit bringt Rat.) *Time brings everything to light.* *Time will tell.*
	979	Spare (kaufe) in der Zeit, dann hast du in der Not. (Wer spart, wenn er hat, der hat, wenn er bedarf.) *Better to spare at brim than at bottom.* *Provision in season makes a rich house.*

980 Wer nicht kommt zur rechten Zeit, muß nehmen was da übrigbleibt.
He who comes late lodges ill.

981 Zeit, Ebbe und Flut wartet auf niemand.
Time and tide wait for no man.

982 Zeit ist Geld.
Time is money.

Zerstören 983 Zerstören ist leichter als aufbauen.
It is easier to pull down than to build up.

Zorn 984 Dem Zorne geht Reue auf den Socken nach.
The end of passion is the beginning of repentance.

985 Zorn beginnt mit Torheit und endet mit Reue.
Anger begins with folly and ends with repentance.

Zucht 986 Wie die (gute) Zucht (der Flachs), so die (gute) Frucht (das Garn).
What is bred in the bone will come out in the flesh.

Zufrieden- 987 Zufriedenheit geht über (ist der größte) Reichtum.
heit
Contentment is better than riches.

988 Zufriedenheit wohnt mehr in Hütten als in Palästen.
Content lodges oftener in cottages than in palaces.

Zunge 989 Böse Zungen schneiden schärfer als Schwerter.
The tongue is sharper than the sword.

990 Die Zunge läßt sich nicht meistern.
The tongue is an unruly member.

Zürnen 991 Wer langsam zürnt, zürnt schwer.
Patience provoked turns to fury.

Zusehen 992 Vom Zusehen wird man nicht satt.
The eye is not satisfied with seeing.
Looking at a hill won't move it.

Zwang	993	Zwang hält (währt) nicht lang. *Nothing that is violent is permanent.*
Zwei	994	Können zweie sich vertragen, hat der dritte nichts zu sagen. *Two's company, three's a crowd.*
	995	Wer zwei wetten, muß ein verlieren. *He who chases two hares catches neither.*
	996	Wenn zwei sich streiten, freut sich der dritte. (Wo sich zwei zanken,gewinnt der dritte.) *Two dogs strive for a bone, and a third runs away with it.*
	997	Zwei wissen mehr als einer. *Two heads are better than one.*
Zweig	998	Einen jungen Zweig biegt man, wohin man will. *The young twig is easily bent. Cf. 66*
Zwist	999	Zwist über Liebesleuten hat nicht viel zu bedeuten. *Lovers' quarrels are soon mended. Cf. 760*
Zwölf	1000	Zwischen zwölf und Mittag kann noch viel geschehen. *There's many a slip 'twixt the cup and the lip.* *Between promising and performing, a man may marry his daughter. Cf. 858*

BIBLIOGRAPHY

Angress, R.K. *Early German Epigram. A Study in Baroque Poetry.* Lexington, Kentucky: University Press of Kentucky, 1971.

Arnaud, P. & Béjoint, H. *Vocabulary and Applied Linguistics.* London: Macmillan, 1992.

Bausinger, Hermann. *Formen der Volkpoesie.* Berlin: Erich Schmidt, 1968.

Bebermeyer, Gustav. "Sprichwort." *Reallexikon der deutschen Literaturgeschichte.* Eds. Paul Merker & Wolfgang Stammler. Berlin: Walter de Gruyter, 1928-29. III, 281-287.

Benas, B.L. "On the Proverbs of European Nations." *Proceedings of the Literary and Philosophical Society of Liverpool.* no. 32 (1877-78).

Braun, Peter & Krallmann, Dieter. "Inter-Phraseologismen in europäischen Sprachen." *Internationale Studien zur interlingualen Lexikologie und Lexikographie.* Eds. P. Braun, Burkhard Schaeder & Johannes Volmert. Tübingen: Max Niemeyer, 1990. 74-86.

Carter, Ronald. *Vocabulary. Applied Linguistic Perspectives.* London: Allen & Unwyn, 1987.

Champion, Selwyn Gurney. *Racial Proverbs: A Selection of the World's Proverbs, Arranged Linguistically with Authoritative Introductions to the Proverbs of 27 Countries and Races.* London: Routledge & Kegan, 1963.

Cherkaskii, Mark Abramovich. "Versuch der Konstruktion eines funktionalen Modells eines speziellen semiotischen Systems (Sprichwörter und Aphorismen)." *Semiotischen Studien zum Sprichwort. Simple Forms Reconsidered I.* Eds. P. Grzybek & W. Eismann. Tübingen: Gunter Narr, 1984. 366-377.

Claeys, Patricia Francesca. *Theoretical and Translational Aspects of Phraseology.* MA Thesis. University of New Brunswick, 1989.

Collinson, W.E. "Some German and English Idioms, with a Note on the Definition of the Term 'Idiom.'" *German Life and Letters.* 11 (1957-58), 266-269.

Cowie, Murray, Aiken. *Proverbs and Proverbial Phrases in the German Works of Albrecht von Eyb.* Diss. University of Chicago, 1942.

Dundes, Alan. *Life is Like a Chicken Coop Ladder. A Portrait of German Culture Through Folklore.* New York: Columbia University Press, 1984.

Esser, Wilhelm Martin. "Deutsch-französisch Parallelen in Redenwendung, Sprachbild und Sprichwort. Beobachtungenzu den Schweirigkeiten einer nationalen Charakteristik." *Muttersprache.* 79 (1969), 204-217.

Gerr, Elke. *4000 Sprichwörter und Zitate.* München: Humboldt, 1989.

Grauberg, Walter. "Proverbs and Idioms: Mirrors of National Experience?" in *Lexicographers and their Works.* Ed. G. James. Exeter, U.K.:University of Exeter Press, 1989. 94-99.

Grigas, Kazys. "Das internationale Sprichwort." in *Patarliu Paraleles.* Vilnius:Vaga, 1987.

Grzybek, Peter. "Foundations of Semiotic Proverb Study." *Proverbium* 4 (1987). 39-85.

_____ . "How to Do Things with Some Proverbs: zur Frage eines parömischen Minimums." in *Semiotischen Studien zum Sprichwort. Simple Forms Reconsidered I.* Eds. P. Grzybek & W. Eismann. Tübingen: Gunter Narr, 1984.

Hattemer, K. & Scheuch, E.K. *Sprichwörter: Einstellung und Verwendung.* Düsseldorf: Intermarket. Gesellschaft für internationale Markt-und Meinungsforschung.

Hausmann, Franz Josef et al. Eds. *Wörterbücher. Ein internationales Handbuch zur Lexikographie.* Berlin: Walter de Gruyter, 1989.

Hellwig, Gerhard. *Zitate und Sprichwörter von A - Z.* München: Bertelsmann Lexikon Verlag, 1974.

Hirsch, E.D. *Cultural Literacy. What Every American Needs to Know.* Boston: Houghton Mifflin, 1987.

Hirsch, E.D., Kett, Joseph, Trefil, James. *The Dictionary of Cultural Literacy: What Every American Needs to Know.* Boston: Houghton Mifflin, 1988.

Kirchner, Oswald R. *Parömiologische Studien (Zwei kritische Beiträge).* rpt. ed by Wolfgang Mieder. Bern: Peter Lang, 1984.

Kremer, Edmund P. *German Proverbs and Proverbial Phrases with their English Counterparts.* Stanford: Stanford University Press, 1955.

Mieder, Wolfgang. *Deutsche Sprichwörter in Literatur, Politik, Presse und Werbung.* Hamburg: Helmut Buske, 1983.

_____ (ed.). *Deutsche Sprichwörterforschung des 19 Jahrhunderts.* Bern: Peter Lang, 1984.

_____ . *English Proverbs.* Stuttgart: Philipp Reclam, 1988.

_____ . *International Proverb Scholarship. An Annotated Bibliography.* NY: Garland Publishing, 1982. *Supplement I* (1990). *Supplement II* (1993).

_____ . *Investigations of Proverbs, Proverbial Expressions, Quotations and Clichés. A Bibliography of Explanatory Essays which Appeared in "Notes and Queries" (1849-1983).* Bern: Peter Lang, 1984.

_____ . "Moderne Sprichwörterforschung zwischen Mündlichkeit und Schriftlichkeit." in L. Röhrich & E. Lindig, eds. *Volksdichtung zwischen Mündlichkeit und Schriflichkeit.* Tübingen: Gunter Narr.

_____ . "Neues zur demoskopischen Sprichwörterkunde." *Proverbium* 2 (1985).

_____ . "Paremiological Minimum and Cultural Literacy." in *Wise Words: Essays on the Proverb.* ed. W. Mieder. NY: Garland, 1994.

_____ . *Tradition and Innovation in Folk Literature.*

Hanover/New Hampshire: University Press of New England, 1987.

Mieder W., Dundes A. (eds). *The Wisdom of Many. Essays on the Proverb.* New York: Garland, 1981.

Mieder W., Kingsbury S.A., Harder K.B. *A Dictionary of American Proverbs.* Oxford: OUP, 1992.

O'Rourke, Joseph P. *Toward a A Science of Vocabulary Development.* Hague: Mouton, 1974.

Permiakov G.L. *300 Obshcheupotrebitel'nykh poslovits i pogovorok.* Moskva: Nauka, 1985.

_____. "On the Question of a Russian Paremiological Minimum." English translation by K.J.McKenna in *Proverbium* 6 (1989).

_____. *Paremiologicheskii eksperiment: Materialy dlia paremiologicheskogo minimuma.* Moskva: Nauka, 1971.

_____. *Paremiologicheskii Sbornik.* Moskva, 1978.

Pfeffer, J.A. *The Proverb in Goethe.* New York: Columbia University Press, 1948.

Roy, Claude. 'La sagesse des nations." in id. *L'homme en question.* Paris: Gallimard, 1960. 39-49.

Seiler, Friedrich. *Deutsche Sprichwörterkunde.* München: Beck, 1922.

_____. *Das deutsche Lehnsprichwort.* 4 vols. Halle: Verlag der Buchhandlung des Waisenhauses, 1921-1924.

_____. *Das deutsche Sprichwort.* Strassburg: Karl J. Trübner, 1918.

Simrock, Karl. *Die deutschen Sprichwörter.* rpt. with an introduction by W. Mieder. Stuttgart: Philipp Reclam Jun, 1988.

Wander, K.F.W. *Das Sprichwort, betrachtet nach Form u. Weseb, für Schule u. Leben, als Einleitung zu einem großen volkstümlichen Sprichwörterschatz.* rpt. with an introduction by W. Mieder. Bern: Peter Lang, 1983.

Whiting, Bartlett Jere. *Modern Proverbs and Proverbial Sayings.* Cambridge, Mass.: Harvard University Press, 1989.

Wilson, F.P. *The Oxford Dictionary of English Proverbs.* Oxford: OUP, 1970.

English Key Word Index

Index entries are arranged by *key word*, by which is meant the sequentially first noun most closely associated with the meaning of the proverb and/or having greater linguistic range or frequency. For proverbs without nouns, key words are verbs, adjectives or adverbs used on the basis of the same criteria. All numbers refer to the numbered German proverb entries.

Enjoy these other titles in the Hippocrene Bilingual Proverbs Series . . .

Dictionary of 1000 French Proverbs
by Peter Mertvago
144 pages, 5 ½ x 8 ½
ISBN 0-7818-0400-0 $11.95pb   (146)

Dictionary of 1000 Italian Proverbs
by Peter Mertvago
144 pages, 5 ½ x 8 ½
ISBN 0-7818-0458-2 $11.95pb   (370)

Dictionary of 1000 Polish Proverbs
by Miroslav Lipinski
144 pages, 5 ½ x 8 ½
ISBN 0-7818-0482-5 $11.95pb   (568)

Dictionary of 1000 Spanish Proverbs
by Peter Mertvago
144 pages, 5 ½ x 8 ½
ISBN 0-7818-0412-4 $11.95pb   (254)

. . . and

The Comparative Russian-English Dictionary of
Russian Proverbs & Sayings
by Peter Mertvago
477 pages, 8 ½ x 11
ISBN 0-7818-0424-8 $35.00pb (555)

German-English / English-German Practical Dictionary
35,000 entries 400 pages 5 ½ x 8 ¼
ISBN 0-7818-0355-1 $9.95pb (200)

Mastering German
by A.J. Peck
322 pages 5 ½ x 8 ½
ISBN 0-87052-061-X $11.95pb (514)
Mastering German Cassettes
2 cassettes
ISBN 0-87052-061-X $12.95 (515)

Treasury of German Love Poems, Quotation & Proverbs
edited by Almut Hille
Selections from Schiller, Goethe, Rilke and others.
128 pages, 5 x 7
ISBN 0-7818-0296-23 . $11.95hc (180)
Treasury of German Love Audio Cassettes
2 cassettes
ISBN 0-7818-0360-8 $12.95 (577)